THE 4 STAGES OF A TEAM

"Steve Ritter's book will immediately be part of my go-to collection of resources I use when working with teams. The Team Clock® methodology shared in this book provides an impactful model that understands the dynamic nature of teams and provides tools to help make them more successful. Case studies across industries prove the value of the approach, that is further supported by empirical data from so many success stories. The writing has a compassionate and optimistic tone to help leaders in even the most challenging situations see a path to success."

– Tim Ressmeyer, Ph.D.
Founder, Ressmeyer Partners Leadership Coaching
Author, *The Impact of Confidence: 7 Secrets of Success for the Human Side of Leadership*

"After having engaged in strategic planning for an international medical society and for a large historic community of faith, I had seen how the process could propel an organization towards greater success. I wanted the same for my academic unit. We're a diverse group that includes engineers and designers focused on innovation, clinicians wanting to deliver the best healthcare possible, scientists discovering the secrets of nature, and staff trying to navigate many disparate needs. At the start there was much skepticism, a not unexpected consequence of participants whose exacting natures make for their career successes. What was remarkable was how quickly the skeptics became believers as they understood the concepts behind Team Clock® and could see directly how their thoughtful input made for effective work together in a direction aligned with their talents and passions. With this book, Steve lays out the fundamentals of Team Clock® and narrates cases with clear analytics of how teams moved towards success by understanding the cyclical patterns of organizational dynamics and how those patterns could be used to progress. Although I've been lucky enough to have Steve lead us in our strategic planning, I learned much from this enjoyable, informative book."

– CRAIG NIEDERBERGER, M.D.
Clarence C. Saelhof Professor and Head, Department of Urology
University of Illinois at Chicago

"The true value of *The 4 Stages Of A Team* lies in its practicality, but also in that it comes to us already battle tested. Unlike generalized or theoretically derived material, the insights here come from Team Clock's years of immersion in real life problem solving situations entrusted to Mr. Ritter by a wide variety of business clients. The 'Why?' is here, but also the 'How.' These are the right solutions for the complexities of current day interpersonal relationships in commerce and beyond."

– FRANK PORTOLESE
Professor/Musician/Southport Records recording artist

"Wow. The team we've been talking about for years now needs that. There are whole conversations to have about diversity. On our team, we have all sorts of the usual PC diversity stuff, but nobody ever talks about diversity of discipline and bridging gaps and gaining mutual respect between, say, engineers and creatives. Renewal. Yeah."

– FLINT DILLE
Hollywood Screenwriter, Author, *Game Creator - GZP/Ingress/Niantic*

"Everyone knows the importance of working as a team, but few of us know how to accomplish this. I can say from personal experience that the approach set forth in this book works. Following it allowed us to dramatically increase both the productivity and the collegiality of my department."

– MICHAEL MELBINGER
Former Department Chair, Employee Benefits and
Executive Compensation, Winston and Strawn, LLP

"The effective management of a team might seem like second nature, but when you are in the midst of it, it is difficult to accurately assess the dynamics taking place. In *The 4 Stages of a Team* you will learn to step back, accurately assess what stage your team is in, and apply proven methods to correct any negative dynamics or capitalize on positive dynamics to move to the next progressive stage."

— SCOTT MALAGA
VP Consulting, The Marketing Arm

Praise for the Team Clock® method:

"Think hard, really hard, about what it means to join or lead a group of people."
— SETH GODIN
Bestselling Author, *Tribes, Linchpin, This is Marketing*

"Team Clock provides a clear and powerful road map for how people can maximize their relationships to help propel their group to new heights."
— MIKE FEINBERG
Co-Founder, KIPP Schools

"A simple, direct and powerful resource for engaging and leading teams in the new economy."
— MICHAEL FOSTER
Chairman and CEO, Human Capital Institute

"A concise, clear and unique approach to understanding the psychology of teams and how to maximize their performance. A great read for busy executives who care about teamwork."
— ANDY PLEWS
Senior Vice President, Corporate Communications, BMO Financial Group

"A perfect step up for students of team dynamics who are ready for a thought-provoking framework that goes beyond the basic model of forming, storming, norming and performing"

– Professor Julie Hennessy
Clinical Professor of Marketing, Kellogg Graduate School of
Management, Northwestern University

"A wonderful common language for the development of professional learning teams."

Jack Eliot
Co-Director, Midwest Principals Center

THE 4 STAGES

OF A

TEAM

How teams thrive...
and what to do when they don't

STEVE RITTER

For bulk orders, please call 630.832.6155 or email booksales@teamclock.com

Published by Center for Team Excellence.

ISBN 978-0-9890132-3-9

www.CenterforTeamExellence.com

Printed In The United States of America.

– TABLE OF CONTENTS –

– FOREWORD –

Ask people about their most frustrating work experience, and they'll often describe a problem with a team. They might say something like this:

- *"On paper, I guess I was the 'team leader.' In reality, I was just trying to survive day-to-day. They didn't say it, but I know at least half my team thought I was doing a bad job."*
- *"There was a heavy air of disrespect and mistrust that you felt as soon as you entered the office. Sometimes thinking about work caused me to break out into such a heavy sweat that I had to change my clothes."*
- *"I guess the people on my team were good people, for the most part. After all, we were all working in healthcare at a hospital, trying to help people. But somehow, when you put us together, it didn't work."*

People have emotional, visceral reactions when they describe tough team experiences. The inverse is also true. When people describe their most positive work experiences, they often share how much they enjoyed working with their colleagues and all that they accomplished together on a great team.

My personal interest in teams stems in part from a failure I had leading a team when I was a 19-year-old Harvard student. The summer after my sophomore year, I hired and led a staff of six full-time employees for a social impact project, most of them other Harvard students. By the end of the summer, here were some things that had happened:

- I had great relationships with half of the team. The rest I would never talk to again, even if I were to walk right by them on campus. (And I usually say hi to everyone I know.)
- I had fired one-third of the team.

♦   Our team dynamics were so bad, we had to have an outside consultant come in and talk to us about team dynamics. (It only made things worse.)

The thing that bothered me most: I couldn't figure out exactly what had gone wrong. We had worked really hard, averaging 70-plus hours a week. Each person on the team was a nice person outside of the team. Yet, when you put us together, we had tremendous conflict and underperformed.

Years later, I was having lunch with this book's author, and he shared with me that he had developed a model he had used informally to help teams for about 30 years. Steve sketched the model out for me on a napkin in less than two minutes. The simplicity and explanatory power shocked me. *If only I would have known this model early in my life, I would have spared myself and my colleagues so much frustration.*

I implored Steve to share the Team Clock® model with the world so he could empower people to create strong, high-performing teams and spare people the pain of being on dysfunctional ones. We founded The Center for Team Excellence and have since worked with more than 300 teams, including major corporations such as Kraft, Kellogg's and Northwestern Mutual.

Teams are often the most expensive part of an organization, with salaries, benefits and other associated expenses. On a purely business level, I believe this book will help you maximize your return on investment in your teams and drive key metrics such as employee retention.

What excites me most, however, is how this book will help you create the kind of positive, high-performance cultures that you and your colleagues deserve and can be proud of for years to come. *The 4 Stages of a Team* will give you the tools to decode the complexity of teams and create an environment where you and your colleagues thrive. Enjoy!

Mawi Asgedom
CEO, Mawi Learning

– INTRODUCTION –

Stay Stuck or Move Forward

The bullies were unhappy about an outside consultant brought in to fix the broken team. By the time he began assessing what had gone wrong in their university-based hospital department, the six naysayers had already gained a lot of dominance over the 24 other faculty members. Their leader was a tall, internationally respected African-American physician who was unafraid to derail a meeting when she felt her power was threatened.

A year earlier, there had been a change of leadership in the department, with a mixed response from the faculty: A majority were eager for the possibilities of growth, while a vocal minority preferred the leadership style of the outgoing chairman, who, while nice, held few people accountable. With a department divided, the consultant's job was to find some common ground. Often, there are a few basic values (e.g., respect, embracing diversity, commitment to excellence) on which everyone can agree. This exercise would provide a starting point.

In the middle of the first faculty retreat workshop, the leader of the bullies stood up, interrupting the exercise.

"Speaking for all of us, we're all a little tired of these 'Kumbaya, what's your favorite color?' exercises," she said. "They are a waste of our time."

"Really?" the consultant replied. "So, what is your favorite color?"

"Black," she retorted. "You surprised?"

"Actually, I am," the consultant answered. "I would have guessed purple."

"Why purple?" she asked.

"Because you're so passionate," he replied.

The ringleader sat back down, and the workshop resumed. The first effort to impugn the integrity of the facilitator had failed. There would be other tries.

How did it get to this point? The outgoing department chair had been widely considered one of the kindest physicians in the hospital. In a field of competitive peers, he got along with everyone. His tenure as a leader preceded the years when clinical outcomes and financial stewardship became non-negotiable. Grandfatherly leadership had its advantages, but the healthcare industry demanded more. A new generation of leaders was coming of age, and their marker was accountability.

As team members from the Baby Boomer generation stepped away, younger, mid-career talent began filling the vacancies. The new department chair had been heavily recruited from a major academic medical center on the East Coast. She arrived with a reputation for turning around under performing teams. She had no patience for anything mediocre and was armed with best-practice protocols.

The protests began before her first day on the campus. One veteran faculty member had read an article about her love for sweeping change in a recent professional publication. Another had attended a conference where the incoming chair had presented on the topic of cultural transformation in performance expectations for medical faculty. It was clear that significant change would accompany her arrival. In a preemptive strike, a small group of veteran faculty scheduled a meeting with the dean of the medical college to challenge the selection of the outsider. They believed one of their internal peers was more qualified based on her seniority and familiarity with the demographics of the hospital, medical group and local community. They argued that an outsider would not be able to embrace the unique nature of the patient population and that her track record had limited application to the nuances of their market.

The dean listened openly but stood by his decision to welcome a new perspective to the health system. He encouraged the group of protesters to keep him up to speed on any problems arising from the new leader's approach. As a small group of powerful faculty members, they vowed to keep the pressure on.

The new department chair never had a chance. The vocal minority rejected her before she ever had an opportunity to prove herself. They inundated the dean's calendar with complaints and did their best to make life miserable for the incoming chair by disrupting staff meetings and refusing to implement the first round of process changes. While most faculty members were eager to follow the new leader and saw the value in the greater accountability she espoused, a small but powerful group of teammates had chosen to direct their energy toward a concerted effort to get her ousted. The faculty divided into clear factions. Six veterans vocally challenged the chair at every opportunity. The other 24 were mostly younger and had a lot to lose by standing up to the bullies.

The results of the outside consultant's initial assessment were not surprising. Disrespect was tolerated and woven into the norms of the team. Diverse perspectives were not welcomed. Teammates were afraid to innovate for fear of retaliation from the bullies. Change could not move forward because the power of the vocal minority made it unsafe to take risks. The faculty could name the mission, values and vision they wanted, but less than 100 percent accountability would spell doom for these things being successfully implemented. The path forward seemed clear on paper, but the politics of the group would make it impossible to execute.

The consequences of challenging the ringleader were well-known. Anyone foolish enough to stand up to her would be targeted by others who had learned to do her work for her. The tail was wagging the dog. The culture was built on protecting the status quo, regardless of how toxic the environment had become. And unfortunately, one of the consequences of the team's previous culture was that nothing got done with quality or efficiency. Decisions were wrought with politics. Debate was contentious and disrespectful. Valuable energy was consumed managing the fallout of disagreement. Rather than differences in perspective being harnessed to fuel innovation, they were used as weapons. The fact that the workplace was unhealthy was common knowledge. The dysfunction had become normal.

It looked like the workplace bullies had won. Although they made up only 20 percent of the team, nearly everyone was afraid of them. Plus, they now appeared to have the dean's ear.

Sharing the assessment results shined a light on what everyone already knew: The team was broken. And no one knew how to disempower the bullies so the rest of the team could move forward with healthier norms.

At this point, the team had a critical choice: stay stuck or move forward. Oddly, staying stuck was the easier option. Pain was normalized. Moving forward would take resolution. The courage to stand up to the bullies didn't happen until the team acknowledged the dire ramifications of staying stuck. The choice to halt a team's growth would have serious costs:

+ Daily violation of organizational mission and values
+ Weakened productivity because of the distraction of internal politics
+ Failure to innovate and keep pace with best practices
+ Loss of both young and veteran talent
+ Inability to attract and retain a sustainable team because of the palpable tension
+ Long-term damage resulting from a public reputation of dysfunction

With the assessment results on the table, staying stuck would need to become a conscious choice if the bullies were to remain in power. Once the costs of the mutiny were acknowledged, the engaged majority was compelled to take charge. To move forward, the new department chair would need to lead the team in defining the new workplace culture. Clarity and consensus would be needed. Those who wished to get on board would be welcomed if they agreed to behave according to the team's values. Those who preferred to amplify the protest would need to pursue other interests.

The choice to move forward was presented to the team. All but one decided to follow the new leader.

In a tense meeting, the large-font message "Stay Stuck or Move Forward" was projected onto a 6-by-10-foot screen. Team members were invited to remain in the meeting or excuse themselves to a room down the hall. Those staying would immediately get to work on shaping the team's future norms, roles, expectations, values and goals.

The team was given 60 seconds to decide whether to stay or go. For the first 30 seconds, the room was silent and nobody moved. Suddenly, the leader of the bully faction swiveled her chair 180 degrees so that her back was to the rest of the team. Nonverbal communication is sometimes more powerful than verbal messages.

Immediately, the department chair remarked that the act of turning one's back on a team was the equivalent of leaving the room and reminded the lead bully that she now had only 20 seconds to either turn around or leave for real. She turned around with a deep sigh and a roll of her eyes.

She remained silent, verbally and nonverbally, for the next two hours as her teammates hammered out the language and behavioral expectations of a code of conduct that would guide their path forward. For the next month, she was rarely seen in the workplace. Six weeks later, she announced her resignation after a successful

> job search. The team cancer had been successfully self-removed. The remaining physician faculty privately referred to it as a "bully -ectomy."
>
> Of course, there is more to this story. This team had struggled for quite a while before consultants were brought in. There would be additional struggles as they moved forward. These would be managed with new tools and a recipe for healthy teams. The complete story of this team – their challenge, the assessment, actions taken and the outcome – is detailed in Chapter 5.

Running a successful business involves people, processes and products. This book is about the people – written to support teams of people for sustained success. *Team Clock: A Guide to Breakthrough Teams* was designed to introduce a model for effective teaming. That book was the "why." This book, *The 4 Stages of a Team*, is the "how."

In the chapters that follow, you'll learn the four stages that happen in all teams, based on the Team Clock® method. At each stage, you'll discover tools to address challenges that get teams stuck. Understanding these struggles will help you move forward during both prosperity and adversity.

More than 1,000 teams have embraced the Team Clock® method. Team Clock® has been endorsed by internationally recognized leaders in sports, consumer products, professional services, education and healthcare seeking to improve both business results and the health of their organizations. The impact includes:

- Team Clock® was selected as the culture integration model for the largest merger/acquisition of 2010.
- More than 16,000 high school students nationally trained in the Team Clock® method through online leadership courses between 2012 and 2018.
- Team Clock® was established as core curriculum in nationally recognized executive MBA programs at the University of Illinois and

Olivet Nazarene University in 2015.
+ Team Clock® was named "Best in Show" at the 2016 International Association of Business Communicators (IABC) World Conference.

For some teams, the greatest challenge is building a foundation for workplace wellness. For others, the test is to sustain an already healthy organization – rather than fixing something broken, these teams come out of the gate with strength and devote their energy to continuing to thrive in the face of change. Teams like this are often recognized as "best in class."

Throughout this book, stories and case studies from some of these teams, like the one below, will be shared to help you apply best practices with your teams in your own workplace. Although your situation may be playing out in a different industry, we all have similar challenges, so these stories can be applied to all teams.

A BANK LIKE NO OTHER

Nearly 20 years ago, a group of financial services professionals launched the bank of their dreams, one that would focus on meeting the unique needs of private business owners and entrepreneurs. The market difference would be an unyielding attention to treating all employees and customers with respect. Their vision was to build a positive workplace culture from the ground up. In short, happy employees would translate to happy customers. Minimizing turnover and maximizing employee retention would help ensure customer loyalty.

Team Clock® was introduced as a tool to allow collaboration from everyone. Through a series of retreats, workshops, lunchtime trainings and one-on-one coaching sessions, the team was immersed in the Team Clock® principles. The team moved through the frustrations of getting established, the celebrations of trust and connection, the anxieties of innovation, the depletion of change and the renewal of reinvestment. Every challenge was used as an opportunity to grow.

Five years later, Leaders Bank was named the "#1 Best Place to Work in Illinois" by the Illinois Chamber of Commerce and the Society for Human Resources Management. A year later, the bank was recognized as one of "Chicago's 101 Best and Brightest Companies to Work For" by the National Association of Business Resources. The following year, the bank was ranked #51 in *Entrepreneur Magazine's* "Hot 100 Fastest Growing Companies."

The year after that, the bank was one of 35 finalists in the *Wall Street Journal's* "Top Small Workplaces" competition. And the year after that, the bank received the Platinum award from the American Heart Association as one of the country's "Fit Friendly Companies." Finally, a decade after launch, the bank received a Best Practice award as a "Psychologically Healthy Workplace" from the American Psychological Association.

Fueled by a commitment to wellness in the workplace, this team was rewarded repeatedly for its effective response to growth.

CURRENT RESEARCH

Being part of a team is an emotional journey. While intellectual intelligence can be a primary driver of individual performance, emotional intelligence is often the variable that most affects the workings of a team. How we treat each other shapes the norms of the workplace.

An appreciation of differences helps when managing conflicts. Respect and accountability build trust. Psychological safety leads to more creativity and innovation. Flexibility and resilience bring out maturity during stressful times. The science of effective teaming has been rigorously studied in business and higher education settings, and a review of major findings reveals some important themes.

A recent **Google** study cited five key drivers of effective teams:

1. Psychological safety: You can take risks without feeling insecure or embarrassed.
2. Dependability: You can count on each other to do high-quality work on time.
3. Structure and clarity: Goals, roles and execution plans are clear.
4. Meaning of work: Everyone on the team is working on something that is personally important to them.
5. Impact of work: You fundamentally believe the work matters.

A recent **Human Capital Institute** study cited three key drivers of effective teams:

1. Intention: Teams are meaningful, with a clear purpose and defined expectations.
2. Interaction: Skills training helps to ensure positive team dynamics and productivity.
3. Influence: There's an emphasis on effective internal and external team leadership.

A recent **Harvard Business Review** study cited five key drivers of effective teams:

1. Everyone on the team talks and listens equally, keeping contributions brief.
2. Teammates face one another, and their conversations and gestures are energetic.
3. Teammates connect directly with one another – not just with the team leader.
4. Teammates can carry on back-channel or side conversations within the team.
5. The team takes breaks, goes exploring outside the team and brings information back.

A recent **MIT** study cited four key drivers of effective teams:
1. Clear roles and boundaries increase the team's cohesiveness.
2. There's an emphasis on diversity in the group.
3. Meaningful goals fuel the group's motivation.
4. Strong leaders act as the stewards of the team's wellness.

The research is clear: Effective teams have common themes. There's an investment in a meaningful mission and clear norms to guide movement toward the goal. Conflict is navigated constructively. Trust creates a bond of collaboration. Psychological safety and an appreciation of differences support innovation. Change and growth are managed with resilience.

The 4 Stages of a Team will share tools to enhance team norms, mission alignment, conflict resolution, respect, trust, accountability, connection, innovation and change management. Readers can use these action strategies for both immediate impact and long-term culture-building. Then, once a healthy team is established, the task of managing change and sustaining wellness unfolds. Whether it's because of internal changes or a different landscape in the market, teams must always adapt. Some wait until the struggles require intervention, while others anticipate the consequences of growth and get out in front of the change.

FROM FRACTURED TO FOCUSED

Ten years after the largest healthcare merger in the Chicago market, Advocate Healthcare's corporate leadership began to rethink its regionalized business structure. While southern, central and northern clusters of business activity made sense at the time of the merger, many key functions of healthcare delivery had since been streamlined for efficiency. Centralizing leadership now made sense.

However, while it was easy on paper to make a case for centralization, each of the regions had developed its own unique culture over the previous decade. Each regional vice president's leadership style was different, and work processes reflected these distinctions. Communication patterns in each region were embedded in decade-old merger politics. Bringing everyone together for the sake of efficiency would require negotiation, compromise and adaptation.

In the earliest stages of the transition, the natural instincts of protection and competition fueled some conflict. Over time, each regional leader was asked to answer some very basic questions: Why do we do this work? What is the service we provide? How does the way we provide the service differentiate us from our industry competition? What is our goal for a better future?

It was surprisingly easy to get agreement on these questions. The answers became the platform of philosophy, mission, values and vision for the new centralized structure. As long as everyone stayed true to the why, the what, the how and the common objective, the new leadership team would be able to build a culture that included the best aspects of each region.

Clear norms, respectful conflict and shared accountability became the team's fuel for innovation. Change became exciting instead of scary. No matter what lay ahead, they now had a toolkit for team survival.

The following chapters will introduce the application of the Team Clock® model – the "how" – through the experience of clients from *investing, trusting, innovating* and *distancing* teams who have adopted Team Clock® to transform their organizations over the last decade. Take a close look at each stage in terms of the problem identification (What does a team at each stage look like?), key pain points (What are the symptoms of struggle?), interventions (What specific actions are helpful?) and outcomes (What will move the team forward?).

A detailed description of the Team Clock® model is provided in

Chapter 1 for your reference. A quick read of *Team Clock: A Guide to Breakthrough Teams* will also provide a basic understanding of the methodology. In the meantime, enjoy the stories and case studies from colleagues in teams like yours who have successfully tackled the problems we all face.

– CHAPTER 1 –

A Toolkit for Team Survival

WHAT IS TEAM CLOCK®?

All relationships travel through cycles of growth and change. Whether it's two people in a partnership, a team of people with a common goal or an organization with a mission, the living entity evolves through predictable stages. At the beginning, teammates *invest* in a future together and carefully define its direction. As the team becomes close and discovers how to work out differences, *trust* becomes the fuel for connection. The foundation of shared values and accountability becomes a platform for *innovation*. This exploration creates change, which requires some *distancing* to adjust to what has been lost, refuel, and adapt to the new circumstances.

Once the team has coped with the change, partners return to another cycle as they deepen their *investment*, strengthen their *trust*, invite more daring *innovation* and *distance* again to manage the next round of growth.

Each of these stages has unique characteristics. Strengths and weaknesses developed in each stage are delivered to the next stage. Healthy teams tend to get healthier, while sick teams tend to get sicker. It takes deliberate effort to stay on a path to sustained team wellness.

The Team Clock® model was conceived in 1980 as an alternative to the 1965 *Tuckman Forming-Storming-Norming-Performing* theory. Rather than viewing a team as a time-limited task group with a beginning, middle and end, the Team Clock® model views teams as ever-evolving, living entities that repeatedly cycle through stages of investment, trust, innovation and distancing, only to reinvest and repeat the cycle.

Imagine 12 hours of a clock, where each hour represents a phase of a team's development. The clock is always circling the dial as teams address the challenges of four key stages:

THE TEAM CLOCK® MODEL

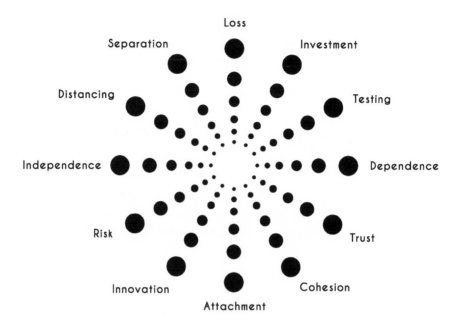

STAGE 1: *Investment*

Whether a team is beginning a project or entering a new season, getting off on the right foot is vital. Future performance will reflect any strengths or weaknesses built into the team's chemistry. Clarity about team norms and goals lays the groundwork for managing conflict successfully.

1:00 – Investment in the team's norms, mission and values establishes a foundation.

2:00 – Testing conflict highlights the differences that will be needed later when the team is ready to innovate.

3:00 – Dependence connects teammates as they commit to collaborating toward common goals.

STAGE 2: *Trust*

Once teammates learn to depend on each other, the work becomes a reflection of this engagement. It only takes one bad apple to spoil a bushel. In an environment that encourages connection and models respect, colleagues hold themselves and each other accountable.

>**4:00 – Trust** grows when teammates are accountable to the agreed-upon norms, mission, values and vision.
>**5:00 – Cohesion** develops as teammates grow more connected through respect, collaboration and shared experience.
>**6:00 – Attachment** is the result of sustained mission alignment, successful conflict management, trust and connection, which forms a platform for growth.

STAGE 3: *Innovation*

Taking risks is contrary for teams that value stability. Hearing diverse points of view can be unsettling for some teammates. Yet, risk-taking and diversity may be the best fuel for innovation. Teams rarely thrive by staying the same. Most succeed by daring to be different.

>**7:00 – Innovation** is made possible by psychological safety and comfort with growth and change. This allows teammates to harness their differences as strengths.
>**8:00 – Risk** must be tolerated to move away from the status quo and toward an unknown future together.
>**9:00 – Independence** allows teammates to stretch themselves while relying on the foundation built in the first two stages. The result is change.

STAGE 4: *Distancing*

Staying poised and resilient under pressure is especially difficult when teammates are deeply invested in each other and the outcome of their work. Powerful emotional reactions usually color a team's response to a crisis. Adapting to new circumstances is easier once a team has had a chance to process what has been lost. Letting go of the past helps teammates refocus on what's ahead.

10:00 – Distancing is a healthy reaction to the change the team has created. This allows teammates to move away from the way it has always been and evaluate new circumstances.

11:00 – Separation from the status quo is necessary to let go of people and processes that won't be moving forward with the change.

12:00 – Loss begins with mourning the disappearance of past connections so the team can refocus on the new situation and reinvest in the next cycle of development.

KEY PRINCIPLES

Principle 1: The clock keeps turning: Cycles are natural for all living things. Moving from stage to stage is the key to growth, even when teams get stuck in predictable places. It's easy to get stuck in each stage. Consider the reasons teams are likely to get stuck:

+ Investment: *Rebuilding a team is hard work after the depletion of a loss.*
+ Trust: *Connection feels good, and it's hard to sacrifice safety for the risks of innovation.*
+ Innovation: *It's scary to be out on a limb trying something new when the outcome is unknown.*
+ Distancing: *Moving away from something familiar and valued exhausts energy. Everyone takes their own time to heal after a loss, disappointment, rejection or failure.*

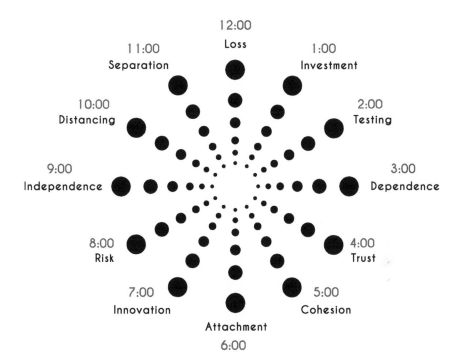

Principle 2: Opposites attract: The challenges in each stage of the clock are powerfully influenced by those on the opposite side. Strength on one side creates strength on the other side. Weakness on one side leads to weakness on the other.

> **1:00 Investment** affects 7:00 Innovation which, in turn, affects future investment.
> **2:00 Testing** affects 8:00 Risk which affects future testing.
> **3:00 Dependence** affects 9:00 Independence which affects future dependency.
> **4:00 Trust affects** 10:00 Distancing which affects future trust.
> **5:00 Cohesion** affects 11:00 Separation which affects future cohesion.
> **6:00** Attachment affects 12:00 Loss which affects future attachment.

Consider the examples in your life. The greater the attachment, the greater the loss. The stronger the commitment to dependency, the stronger the platform for independence. The deeper the investment, the more daring the innovation. The more powerful the trust, the more meaningful the goodbye.

WHY IT WORKS AND WHY IT'S UNIVERSAL

The Team Clock® model has been tested by hundreds of teams in a variety of industries, including global corporate consumer product companies, nationally recognized professional service firms, championship sports teams, leading colleges and universities, and groundbreaking healthcare organizations.

People are people. Relationships are relationships. Teams are teams. The recipe for healthy relationships and effective teams is universal:

Stage 1: Investment	Invest in common goals, healthy norms and constructive conflict.
Stage 2: Trust	Build trust through accountability, respect and connection.
Stage 3: Innovation	Harness differences and take smart risks to innovate.
Stage 4: Distancing	Respond to change by mourning what's lost and embracing what's new.

This approach works in any industry. The product or service your team creates has the best chance of succeeding when the team is healthy, strong, ambitious and adaptable.

Teams are made up of humans. Humans interact in ways that cause struggle. Thus, the value proposition is simple:

THE VALUE PROPOSITION

By identifying and addressing the obstacles interfering with performance, teams can spend more time focusing on their work and less time on the politics of their workplace.

Unchecked organizational politics take away from the team's performance. The less time and energy consumed by workplace politics, the more focused and engaged employees will be with their job responsibilities. Teams that succeed at this exhibit the most magnetic recruitment, the highest morale, the most productivity, the most creative innovation, the most resilient adaptation to change and the best employee retention.

SYMPTOMS OF STRUGGLE

The ideal team flows from challenge to challenge, moving over, under, around or through obstacles. Team members understand the purpose of their struggle and keep working on the problem. Because all living things move through predictable cycles, each transition provides an opportunity to get stuck.

Whether it's to re-establish direction, build connection, push growth or manage change, halting the team's progress is a natural reaction to struggle. The goal is to keep the team moving even when there's an urge to stop. Let's look at the four most likely stuck-points:

STAGE 1: *Investment*

During the Investment Stage, teams are re-establishing their direction after a transition. This is a labor-intensive stage of a team's growth, so frustration is a common emotion. The team wants to forge ahead, but the structure of the team needs to be built or rebuilt.

Typically, this stage is marked by role confusion and conflict. As differences are negotiated, mission, values, vision, goals and norms are clarified. Whatever gets re-established in this stage – whether it's healthy or sick – gets woven into the fabric of the team culture until some other significant change triggers another reboot.

STAGE 2: *Trust*

The foundation that was built in the Investment Stage gets tested in the Trust Stage. Because teammates are growing more connected, the stakes are higher if trust is broken for some reason, big or small. Every team interaction either strengthens or weakens trust. Teammates either follow through with commitments or they don't. Colleagues are either respectful and professional or they're not. Co-workers either hold themselves accountable or they let the rest of the team down.

At this stage, teams rise and fall together. When any teammate thrives, everyone benefits. When someone fails, the whole team suffers. The symptoms of struggle in the Trust Stage include a breakdown of psychological safety, tolerance of disrespect, lack of accountability and weak interpersonal connections. Teams are unlikely to take the risk to innovate (which comes in the next stage) if trust has been compromised.

STAGE 3: *Innovation*

Teams are ready to explore, experiment, discover and create when the vision is clear and trust is strong. While everyone agrees on the destination, there may be many paths to get there. One of the delayed benefits of managing conflict successfully is an appreciation of difference.

A diversity-friendly and risk-tolerant workplace is a rich garden for innovation. However, if the environment is not safe for taking risks, teammates will be restrained by caution. The symptoms of struggle in the Innovation Stage include fear of punishment and careful loyalty to the status quo. Employees who are afraid of a punitive response from leadership are unlikely to stretch themselves. Fear immobilizes the willingness to try new things.

STAGE 4: *Distancing*

The Distancing Stage is focused on coping. Innovation sparks change. As exciting as change can be, it takes a toll on most teams. Whether positive or negative, managing change requires letting go of the old and adjusting to the new.

Living things seek sameness and stability. Growing things adapt. Adapting consumes energy. It's much easier to stay the same. It's normal to feel depleted physically and emotionally when going through a transition.

Some teammates might be unwilling to embrace the new circumstances. Resistance to change is both normal and, in some cases, healthy. Slowing down the process can help the team prepare for what's next.

Everyone heals at a different pace, and it's difficult to accept new conditions when the team's strength is sapped. Like a night's sleep or a tree's dormancy in the winter, the Distancing Stage offers a chance to let go, regroup, refuel and refocus.

TEAMS ARE ALWAYS EVOLVING

Teams thrive in cycles, not straight-line trajectories. Whether it's a short-term task group or a lifelong commitment, team dynamics repeat as teammates manage the challenges of coming together and building something new, tolerating closeness, managing growth and embracing change. As teams move through their lifespans, they repeat each stage over and over, getting more mature each time. The good news is that teams have many chances to reinvest.

A renewal occurs whenever a teammate is added or subtracted. The subtle changes in team chemistry are most noticeable when talent is added or someone leaves. The hierarchy adjusts to the new brand of energy being infused or deleted. Friendships are either strengthened or strained. The ecosystem resets its balance.

A renewal occurs whenever a conflict gets resolved. Tension demands resolution. There is a natural desire for peace when a team is in conflict or struggles to solve a problem. Solutions give way to another round of discovery. Teams that continuously create and resolve tension are always growing.

A renewal occurs whenever an innovation alters the work of the team. Impasses are gifts for teams that thrive on invention. The act of solving a previously unsolvable problem boosts the energy of a team like nothing else. The pain of stretching capacity and resources has a wonderful payoff when the struggle opens new pathways.

A renewal occurs after the celebration of a success or the disappointment of a failure. A win is not the ending. Success becomes a temporary benchmark upon which to evolve. Likewise, a failure doesn't end the game. It just changes the strategy and direction for keeping the game going.

A renewal occurs every time the team's goals are redefined. Course corrections are dramatic responses to the realization that a plan isn't working. Problem-solving includes permission to rethink direction. We define the challenge, consider options, weigh pros and cons, choose the best route and evaluate outcomes. When the outcomes don't address the challenge, we go back to the drawing board and re-evaluate.

Think of a team as a marriage going through many phases. At each stage of a relationship, investment priorities shift, trust strengthens (or weakens), the tolerance for risk adjusts and the direction of the relationship is recalibrated. These subtle changes in team dynamics continue through the life of the relationship.

Teams come in all shapes and sizes. Long marriages are simple examples of the subtle changes couples navigate as they adjust to each other's growth and the changes in their environment. With each phase, partners must recalibrate direction.

A MARRIAGE TAKES MANY FORMS

Jim and Elizabeth got married at a young age, 21. While technically adults, they were playing house. Fresh out of college, they had minimal responsibility and plenty of freedom. Days were spent in entry-level jobs, while nights and weekends were packed with fun.

Everything changed when kids came along. Now there was precious cargo on board. The wild weekends were replaced with family activity. Elizabeth noticed that Jim drove more carefully with a baby strapped into a car seat.

The stakes grew higher when the kids became teenagers. Health and safety concerns now dominated decisions about freedoms and privileges. Mistakes could be costly. The investments of time and money were now fully devoted to preparing the kids for a launch into adulthood.

As Jim and Elizabeth's life savings poured into their children's college educations, they got reacquainted with being alone together in the house. Not unlike the beginning of their marriage, they were now free to spend evenings and weekends doing something other than shuttling their kids to soccer games and piano recitals.

Of course, the kids boomeranged back as they finessed their transitions to adulthood. As soon as Jim and Elizabeth had reclaimed their time and space, the kids moved their lifestyles and belongings back into the home. Jim and Elizabeth adjusted their priorities to accommodate their adult children until the kids were finally ready to make it on their own.

Once the kids successfully executed their own marriages and careers, Jim and Elizabeth settled into a new version of their union. The financial and parenting responsibilities that had driven most of their priorities had passed. They now had the discretion to spend their time and money on more selfish goals. Travel, entertainment and home renovation returned to the marital agenda.

Grandparenting added a new twist. The chance to shape the life of their children's children infused new energy into the family. Watching their kids learn how to be parents was a joy. Acting as consultants when needed was far easier than being solely responsible for the well-being of this new generation of precious cargo.

Retirement changed everything. The interests and activities previously reserved for free time now expanded to daily norms. Jim and Elizabeth established a new rhythm. They learned when to stay apart and when to come together, as some of their interests were in common, while others diverged.

Aging, of course, came with the expected litany of medical issues. Caretaking gradually defined the priorities of a marriage that had enjoyed more than five decades of partnership. All that had been invested and risked over the years provided a rich connection for managing both endings and new beginnings.

Imagine the cyclical changes that might define a healthy 50-plus-year marriage:

Stage 1 (Investment)	"Playing house"
Stage 2 (Trust)	"Adding kids"
Stage 3 (Innovation)	"Kids become teens"
Stage 4 (Distancing)	"Kids leave home"
Stage 1 (Investment)	"Kids boomerang back temporarily"
Stage 2 (Trust)	"Alone together again, but older"
Stage 3 (Innovation)	"Grandparent-hood"
Stage 4 (Distancing)	"Retirement"
Stage 1 (Investment)	"Until we meet again"

At each stage, the way the couple invests is different. At each stage, the depth of trust and connection changes. At each stage, the risk tolerance adjusts to the precious cargo on board (kids). At each stage, loss and reinvestment are handled with more maturity.

Teams go through similar lifespans. Team dynamics are constantly changing. Team Clock® is not a single-use intervention.

- There are people changes (talent turnover, succession, promotion, reassignment, opportunity, tragedy).
- There are process changes (market shifts, financial obstacles, new business priorities).
- There are developmental changes (new team formation, crisis response, resistance to interdependence, inconsistent appetite for growth, maturity differences, psychopathology, toxic work environment).

When teams are running smoothly, they transition from stage to stage without much noise. It's when teams struggle or get stuck that symptoms arise. As with any living thing, the purpose of the symptom is to draw attention to a problem. And each stage of the team's evolution has predictable symptoms.

ASSESSING PAIN POINTS

Most teams know what stage they're navigating without a formal assessment. If you're feeling frustrated, your team is most likely in the Investment Stage. If you're feeling safe and satisfied, your team is probably enjoying the Trust Stage. If you're fearful or anxious, your team is probably in the Innovation Stage. And if you are depleted, your team is most likely going through a change in the Distancing Stage. The advantage of a formal team assessment is that it can target exactly what's playing out in each stage.

A team in the Investment Stage might be struggling with norms, boundaries or role clarity. On the other hand, it might be wrestling with team mission, values and vision where not everyone is aligned. Likewise, the team might be experiencing conflict and having trouble coming to a resolution.

A team in the Trust Stage might be struggling with respect or professionalism. It might also be suffering from a lack of accountability. A team in this stage could also be experiencing a lack of togetherness.

A team in the Innovation Stage might be enduring an intolerance of differences. It might just be risk-avoidant.

A team in the Distancing Stage could be mourning the loss of a teammate or a failed venture. It might also be having difficulty embracing the new circumstances arising out of a recent change or a prolonged transition.

In addition to revealing strengths and weaknesses and the specific nuances of what's affecting a team at that moment, a team assessment will measure the togetherness of the team. Some teams are marked by common ground and consensus. Other teams have outlier members with different perspectives. Still other teams are divided into factions (us vs. them, new guard vs. old guard, legacy vs. acquired, etc.). It's helpful to know how pervasive a strength or a weakness might be on a team. Does everyone feel the same way, or is the issue limited to a select few?

THE TEAM CLOCK® ONLINE ASSESSMENT

Asking employees to take 15 minutes to complete a 40-question online survey (see Chapter 6: Next Steps for Achieving Breakthrough Teams) will provide a window to the inner workings of your team. Once everyone has completed the survey, the leadership team receives a 24-page report detailing *mean scores* of strength and weakness in the key domains of each of the four stages of the team. Deeper insights are revealed through *standard deviation* scores that show team consensus, outlier opinion or factions in each of the four stages of the team.

The Team Clock® summary report shows team strengths, weaknesses, consensus and disparity of opinion in each stage of the team's life cycle. Because the dynamics driving team performance aren't always obvious, the summary report also sorts the data across stages revealing the seven strongest strengths, the seven weakest weaknesses, the seven greatest areas of consensus opinion and the seven areas of greatest disparity in perspective.

Often, the factors most influencing the spirit and morale of the team are buried a little deeper in the metrics. For instance, even if the No. 1 weakness of the team is from the Investment Stage section of questions, it might stem from the fact that five of the seven lowest scores are in the Distancing Stage. The difficulty in the investment stage might be a direct result of the struggle the team is managing with change.

TEAM CLOCK™
ONLINE ASSESSMENT
"Instant insights to propel your team."

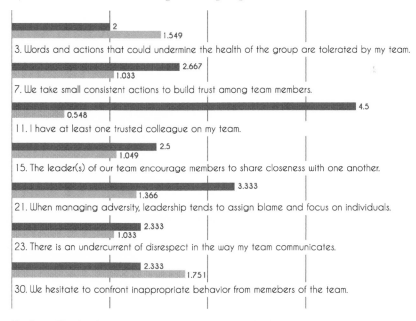

The Team Clock® online assessment shows mean and standard deviation metrics in each stage.

Likewise, a team might have a high mean score in the question, "I have a trusted colleague on the team." However, if the team shares an opinion that "there is an undercurrent of disrespect on the team," that high trust score might be revealing pairs of teammates commiserating about the rest of the team. Each report reveals the unique dynamics that characterize the subtle human interactions on each team in the moment of measurement captured by the survey.

The summary report also includes recommendations. For most teams, it's easy to name the problem, and the online assessment provides statistical validation of common sense observations. Most leaders already know what's weak and strong with their teams. They don't always know what to do about it. The Team Clock® summary report offers short-term and long-term tactics for addressing the vulnerabilities measured in the online survey.

DO IT YOURSELF

Even without a formal assessment, it's easy to see what's happening on a team just by asking a few simple questions. With the understanding that high-performing teams must stay strong through multiple cycles of all four stages, asking these questions will help leaders identify current obstacles or opportunities.

Each of the following 10 questions represents a key domain of team wellness.

- ☐ Are our day-to-day interactions productive, efficient and true to our values?
- ☐ Is our team mission clear, and is everyone on board?
- ☐ Do teammates handle conflict and differences of opinion with maturity?
- ☐ Do teammates connect and collaborate?
- ☐ Is our workplace a trusting and respectful environment?
- ☐ Do teammates hold themselves/each other accountable consistently?

☐ Are we supported in sharing new ideas and perspectives?

☐ Does the organization support exploration and discovery when solving problems?

☐ Are there any unresolved issues keeping the team stuck?

☐ How have we handled significant change recently?

Perform a simple "thumbs-up" or "thumbs-down" response to each question and create a gap analysis. Any "thumbs-up" responses are strengths to be delivered to the team's next stage. Any "thumbs-down" responses are human resources opportunities to strengthen organizational culture. Put your vulnerabilities in triage order, evaluate solutions, implement a tactic and move on to the next priority.

Never rest on your successes. The team is always changing. Neglect only sends the roots of the problem deeper into the culture. Proactively reassess whenever:

✓ Team structure needs clarification (roles/boundaries/norms/mission/values/vision).

✓ Trust, accountability and psychological safety have broken down.

✓ Under performance has derailed the team.

✓ The team needs fuel for innovation.

✓ A significant change has occurred.

✓ The team wants to move from good to great (or from great to greater).

A TOOLKIT FOR THE LIFE OF A TEAM

Your team is always in a stage of development. Knowing where you are and why you are at that stage is the key to moving forward in a healthy way. The goal is to keep moving. The natural tendency of most teams is to get stuck.

It's easy to get stuck when the task of reinvesting is burdensome, or the sense of connection feels comfortable. It's easy to get stuck when innovating is scary, or change depletes the team's energy. Healthy teams keep negotiating these stages throughout their lifespan.

INVESTING TEAMS

Whether you're starting up a new team or reinvesting after a change, it's always valuable to re-anchor your mission and values as the team gets acquainted with its new situation. New cycles are also opportune times to clarify team roles, boundaries and norms.

Of course, this stage of the team's growth is also an important time to practice conflict resolution. Anything that gets woven into the team's fabric in this stage gets delivered to the next stage. Trust, innovation and distancing will all be made easier or more difficult depending on how the team manages this stage.

TRUSTING TEAMS

Perhaps your team has successfully navigated a change, reinvested, and is seeking to build a foundation of trust and connection. Every interaction between every teammate is a chance to strengthen or weaken trust. Accountability (or lack of accountability) can grow or shrink trust.

Whether a big or a small issue, unmanaged breaches of trust undermine the psychological safety of the team, rendering them unlikely to innovate. Ownership of personal connection creates a platform of trust and will support risk-taking when the team seeks to grow.

INNOVATING TEAMS

Often in a team's lifespan, partners are eager to innovate and raise the team to a new level. A foundation of healthy norms, clear roles, productive conflict resolution and reliable trust make it safe for teammates to go out on a limb and explore.

Creativity arises from experimentation, and strong teams can survive a few failures. Often, the learning that follows disappointment becomes the fuel for the next discovery. A certain amount of discomfort is needed for teams to manage this stage and create meaningful change.

DISTANCING TEAMS

Whether it's the transformation your team created or a transition beyond your control, change is constant. Whenever change occurs, teammates must distance from old ways and prepare for new ways. Sometimes this means adjusting to new teammates. Other times, a new team direction drives the change.

Every teammate has different coping skills, whether big or small. Some teammates may be poised and mature, while others might regress and resist. The team is responsible for managing its own change effectively, including both those leading the charge and those who are slower to adapt. The next stage of investment depends on it.

NOW WHAT?

Be deliberate about continuous assessment. Don't wait for something to get the team stuck before evaluating where you are in your lifespan. Always be attentive to where you are, why you're there and where to go next. On a regular basis, make it a habit to ask three questions:

1. Where are we on the Team Clock®?
2. Why are we in this stage?
3. What actions will move us forward?

Many organizations have the human resources talent to address any of the pain points that typically arise in teams. Over the last decade, the Center for Team Excellence has collected a range of best practices from clients and partners who have embraced the Team Clock® methodology. These resources will be discussed in Chapter 6 (Next Steps for Achieving Break-through Teams) and are easily adapted to different team circumstances.

Begin by defining the problem. Study how others have tackled similar challenges. Scale the solution to the scope of your situation. Evaluate the outcome against desired results. Repeat as needed as your team moves around the clock from stage to stage.

THE TEAM CLOCK® MODEL

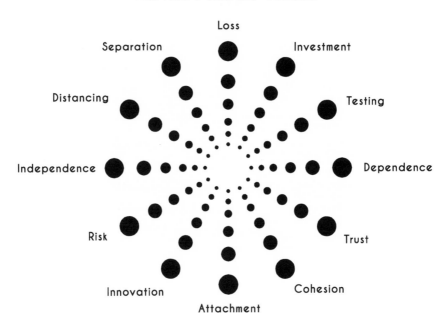

– CHAPTER 2 –

Investing Teams

WHAT THE INVESTING TEAM LOOKS LIKE

Teammates contribute their individual energies to a team, agree to collaborate and commit to a vision for the future. Team norms are negotiated. The organization's "way" of doing things is established. Alignment with a common mission and set of values is achieved. Conflict is acknowledged as a professional and productive way to embrace differences.

While investment rarely seems urgent, teams that invest up front enjoy large dividends later. Teams that invest at a high level create a foundation for future trust, connection, collaboration, innovation and adaptability. Teams that fail to invest may lack meaningful norms, may have little commitment to common goals and may experience destructive (or absent) conflict. Often, unhealthy norms are baked into the team culture, resulting in an undercurrent of disrespect and lack of psychological safety.

KEY PAIN POINTS AND BLIND SPOTS

KEY PAIN POINT	BLIND SPOT
Unhealthy team norms	Disrespect is tolerated.
Lack of alignment with team mission, values and vision	Teammates undermine each other with competing goals and priorities.
Unproductive or destructive conflict	Problems accrue rather than achieving resolution.

HOW TO OVERCOME THEM

KEY PAIN POINT: *Unhealthy Team Norms*

A solid foundation of team norms creates a sustained investment in the health and wellness of the internal culture. Take a moment to name the strengths and gaps in your group as you consider these pillars of a healthy organizational wellness:

- ✓ **Mission/Values/Vision:** A clear sense of purpose and direction fills the workplace.
- ✓ **Open communication:** Honest and transparent exchanges build trust and provide a foundation for successful problem-solving.
- ✓ **Customer focus:** An extraordinary focus on the customer builds long-term relationships and a reason for partnership.
- ✓ **Family-like culture:** Genuine care and concern for co-workers creates a sense of community and a pitch-in spirit.
- ✓ **Sustainability:** Leadership takes a long view of the business so that it can thrive in both prosperous and challenging economies.
- ✓ **Learning and development:** The organization invests in the career paths of employees by customizing projects, resources and networking opportunities that align with the employees' strengths and professional interests.
- ✓ **Succession planning:** The organization creates bench strength to allow future leaders to be groomed from within.
- ✓ **Teamwork:** Collaboration holds teammates together, promotes new ideas and generates fuel for innovation.
- ✓ **Wellness:** The organization has a holistic approach to healthy lifestyles, stress reduction and work/life balance and therefore enjoys a return on investment in terms of employee productivity.
- ✓ **Stewardship:** Employees think and act like owners and are committed to the long-term success of the organization.

CONDUCT A QUICK GAP ANALYSIS

Below are the criteria by which employers of choice are often measured. *Please circle the number that best reflects your perspective on the organization's status in each category.* **Range: "10" represents complete organizational wellness and "0" represents the most need for resources and improvement.**

10   9   8   7   6   5   4   3   2   1   0

Mission/Values/Vision: The organizaion is driven by clear values and a sense of mission/vision that permeates the culture, is shared by everyone and serves as a unifying purpose.
10   9   8   7   6   5   4   3   2   1   0

Open communication: Honest and transparent communication creates trust, enahnces commitment and encourages innovation.
10   9   8   7   6   5   4   3   2   1   0

Customer focus: There is an extraordinary focus on the client and an emphasis on building long-term relationships. These organizations take pride and purpose from participating in events and issues outside of the workplace in the communities in which they live.
10   9   8   7   6   5   4   3   2   1   0

Family-like culture: Leadership has intentionally created a sense of community within the organization.
10   9   8   7   6   5   4   3   2   1   0

Sustainability: Leadership takes a long view of the business in order to thrive in both prosperous and challenging economies.
10   9   8   7   6   5   4   3   2   1   0

Employee Learning & Development: The organization supports career path engagement by taking a comprehensive approach to developing employees.
10   9   8   7   6   5   4   3   2   1   0

Succession Focus: The organization invests in their workforce believes that most of their future leaders are already working in the company.
10   9   8   7   6   5   4   3   2   1   0

Teamwork: Teamwork is considered a core competency. Collaboration holds teams together and helps motivate action toward achieving goals. Teams are recognized and rewarded for their accomplishments.
10   9   8   7   6   5   4   3   2   1   0

Focus on Wellness: There is a holistic approach to supporting balanced and healthy lifestyles, reducing stress, and organizational stweradship.
10   9   8   7   6   5   4   3   2   1   0

Stewardship: Employees act like owners and are committed to the long-term success of the organization.
10   9   8   7   6   5   4   3   2   1   0

Infuse these norms into the team, starting with the gaps you identified in your assessment. Conduct training sessions on interpersonal communications, conflict management and delegation. Teach teammates how to solve problems.

Discuss communication styles and productive ways to handle conflict. Plan relationship-building activities with your team to support a trusting workplace environment. Commit to an ongoing gap analysis of the pillars of organizational wellness and build a strategic plan to continuously strengthen areas of weakness.

Over time, organizations that build a strong foundation of norms create a platform to support trust, accountability, innovation and effective management of change so the team can deliver the strategic goals of the business. This is particularly important during periods of workplace stress when healthy norms must become the glue that holds teammates together. Once rooted, the norms of the business stay the same when everything else is changing.

KEY PAIN POINT: *Lack of Alignment With Team Mission, Values and Vision*

Healthy organizations are built on a platform of philosophy, mission, values and vision that serves as a guide for day-to-day interactions. Discuss team vision with everyone's participation. Document the themes of these exchanges while inviting respectful disagreement. Draft a vision statement reflecting these conversations.

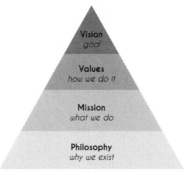

At the base of the pyramid is the **philosophy statement** answering the question, "Why do we exist?" This is a global statement asking teammates to identify the central-most reason they do the work they do each day. Capture the factors that drive your purpose for investing in a team. Consider these examples:

"We strive to conserve the planet's resources."
"We seek to make a difference in the lives of others."
"We are committed to eliminating injustice in the world."
"We exist to help students become lifelong learners who contribute to society."
"We embrace curiosity as a path to discovery, innovation, and problem-solving."
"We aim to create financial security for individuals, families, organizations and communities."

Atop the philosophy statement sits the **mission statement** answering the question, "What do we do?" This is the primary work of the organization. Each teammate lends talent to making the mission possible. Regardless of their role, everyone on the team is linked by a common direction. Here are some example mission statements:

"We support sustainable environments through reuse and recycling."
"We connect people with resources to promote self-determination."
"We confront prejudice and discrimination through community activism."
"We create meaningful learning experiences to engage and motivate all learners."
"We fund start-up businesses that provide creative solutions to global problems."
"We provide investment and insurance solutions to expand the wealth of our clients."

The foundation of philosophy and mission supports a **value statement** that answers the question, "How do we do our work?" The character of the workplace is defined by these values. Often, employees are attracted to a team because of the way the work gets performed. Employers seek talent that fits this value profile and is therefore most likely to produce results. Here are some examples of value statements:

"Our actions will be guided by stewardship and sustainability."
"Professionalism and respect will define the character of our work."
"We are driven by an unwavering commitment to quality and excellence."
"Our work will be marked by transparent communication and professional collaboration."
"Hope, enthusiasm and optimism will steer all decisions and business development activities."
"The four pillars of integrity, ethics, trust and accountability support all client relationships."

Finally, a **vision statement** answers the question, "What are our goals?" Most organizations use the vision statement as motivation for continuous improvement. By stretching the goals slightly out of reach, teammates are encouraged to attain new heights. Powered by the foundation of clear philosophy, mission and values, the vision statement describes the ideal future state. Here are some examples:

"Leave the world in better shape for the next generation."
"Eliminate human suffering and the stigma of mental illness in society."
"Empower social justice for all races, colors and creeds across the globe."
"Exert future-focused leadership in the delivery of world-class educational services."
"Continuously redefine the edge of innovation in an evolving culture of business creation."
"Create a lifetime of financial security and prosperity for clients, families and communities."

Draft a vision statement reflecting the philosophy, mission and values of the team. Compare ideas. Once a consensus has been reached, be willing to edit the vision statement as internal culture evolves.

Implement your vision. Once your vision is clear, define roles and responsibilities for individual team members. Make sure to stay true to the team's direction: What are we trying to accomplish? How does each individual fit in the bigger picture? What is each teammate's role? How do we best link these roles together?

Periodically check for alignment. Devote a part of regular staff meetings to sharing anecdotal evidence that the words and actions of teammates truly reflect the philosophy, mission, values and vision that everyone forged together. Be willing to take a step backward if business conditions alter the goals and direction of the organization. Sometimes it helps to call a timeout and revisit the process. As often as possible, share stories reflecting the vision in action.

KEY PAIN POINT: *Unproductive or Destructive Conflict*

Effective conflict resolution is the bedrock of embracing differences. Healthy organizations recognize diversity, in all its forms, as a necessary component of innovation. Having all ideas on the table in an atmosphere of respect enables healthy teams to adapt during challenging times. Listening also makes it easier for others to hear you when it is your turn to speak. Make the resolution of conflict the main priority rather than trying to "win" or "be right."

Strengthening the relationship should always be your highest priority. Stay in the present. Try to let go of grudges based on past resentments so you can see the current situation clearly. Focus on what you can do in the here-and-now to resolve differences.

Choose your battles. Disagreements are emotionally draining, so make sure it's important enough to be worth your valuable time and energy. Practice forgiveness. The lifespan of a conflict is prolonged if you're not willing to forgive. It takes a lot of energy to hold a grudge. There's no need to punish or show the other person what it feels like to be on the receiving end of distress. Know when to let go.

THESE QUESTIONS CAN HELP RESOLVE TEAM CONFLICTS

Can we agree on a definition of the issue?
What would everyone like to see happen?
What would it take for us to be able to move forward?
Are you willing to share the impact this has had on you?
Are you willing to hear my perspective?
What about this situation is most troubling to you?
What's most important to you?

TEAM SKILLS NEEDED FOR SUCCESS

Exchange	Sharing	Negotiation
✓ Trading ideas and resources ✓ Balancing selfish vs. altruistic motives.	✓ Carrying the burdens of others ✓ Giving away sole own-ership of intellectual property	✓ Comparing competing priorities ✓ Promoting the greater good

CASE STUDY: MERGER/ACQUISITION

Challenge	Assessment	Action	Outcome
Global organization seeks to blend disparate cultures after an acquisition.	Significant change in talent and work processes threatens each business unit's ability to stay focused and productive.	Global leaders convene to integrate new corporate mission and vision, participate in team effectiveness training and prepare for the team assessment process.	The merged entity adopts a common language for effective team performance and uses assessment results to create targeted actions to maximize performance.

THE CHALLENGE

Often, the task of blending cultures begins after a merger or acquisition has been concluded. The decision to integrate companies is made upon the faith that both sides can blend their similarities and differences like mature adults. Unfortunately, the human dynamics that fuel struggle are usually beneath the surface when partners size each other up for marriage. Imagine how the new relationship might begin if both sides could see what was hidden.

The acquisition of a European dairy and confectionery business by a large American food giant was more than a merger of brands. Both companies boasted business units in nearly every continent worldwide. Joining forces filled important strategic gaps in each partner's target markets. But disparate organizational cultures were asked to come together, and while each company made similar consumer products, their philosophies, missions, values and visions shared little in common.

The parent company wisely understood the cultural discrepancy and committed to integration. After an intensive study of the history and strategy of each organization, 50 "change leaders" representing 70 countries gathered to put together an integration toolkit designed to merge cultures. As both businesses carefully navigated the global economy, it was clear that effective teaming was no longer just an option for consideration – it was a mandate of fiscal survival.

THE ASSESSMENT

Department by department, each team participated in a baseline assessment measuring employee investment, trust, innovation potential and change management capacity. Because teams were being reconfigured with talent from both feeder organizations, most departments lacked clarity around philosophy, mission, values and vision. The platforms supporting productivity and efficiency lacked clarity. Even though the newly merged entity had defined its corporate vision, work groups across the globe had vastly different challenges and obstacles.

One business unit's mission was to generate innovative product ideas, yet this unit suffered from a long history of punitive reactions if they failed to gain traction in the market. Why would anyone on that team take another risk after watching teammates get slaughtered for daring to be creative? At first glance, this appeared like an innovation problem. At its root, however, this was the failure of the team to align with a mission statement that embraced differences as strengths. Until such alignment was achieved with consistent accountability, it would be unrealistic to expect innovation.

THE ACTION

Leaders gradually settled into their roles in the new organization. The freshly merged entity had determined its strategic direction for the future. The strengths of disparate corporate histories had been blended to fuel a single direction. The most talented employees chose to stay or go based on their buy-in to the new way of doing business. While departments still struggling with change continued to spend energy on the politics of the workplace, teams aligned with their missions were able to devote full attention to their work.

Every business unit was led by a small team of cross-functional specialists (finance, sales, marketing, R&D, human resources, etc.). Beneath each of these leadership teams was a group of 50 to 60 employees. Each of these "smaller" units had its own unique blend of older and newer talent. With 127,000 employees across five continents, team effectiveness metrics varied wildly from business unit to business unit.

THE OUTCOME

Survey metrics unveiled a broad range of opportunities, including mission/values alignment, communication accountability, civility/respect norms, innovation readiness and change management. As each impediment was addressed, team culture was anchored and productivity metrics improved. By mapping team effectiveness scores to business metrics, performance was maximized.

Teams were reassessed 120 days after the original baseline measurement. Change in team effectiveness metrics were correlated with productivity metrics (e.g., pipeline activity, decision speed, profit margins, etc.). As common sense would suggest, the teams with the greatest increase in team metrics also enjoyed the greatest increase in business performance.

APPLICATION

In a merger, once you've validated the financial wisdom of joining forces, it's time to evaluate the strengths and weaknesses each party brings to the table. When each partner is provided a glimpse of the future, it can be a great advantage. There are 10 drivers of cultural wellness that make or break mergers:

Investment Stage

NORMS	Are rules, roles and boundaries clear and consistent? How do we treat each other in the workplace under normal conditions vs. under stressful conditions?
VISION	Is everyone aligned with the mission and values that support the future direction of the new organization?
CONFLICT	Are differences managed with an appreciation for diversity? Can teammates endure the discomfort required for all perspectives to be heard?

Trust Stage

RESPECT	How does the organization respond to words and actions that could undermine the culture?
ACCOUNTABILITY	Beyond follow-through on commitments, are employees true to the stated mission, values and vision when they interact with clients and colleagues?
CONNECTION	Does trust grow or shrink when teammates collaborate? Does the environment enjoy the psychological safety to support growth?

Innovation Stage

USING DIFFERENCES	Can teammates leave the comfort zone of the status quo to explore, experiment, innovate and create?
RISK	What is the organization's appetite for change? Are teammates willing to extend themselves when the future isn't completely clear?

Distancing Stage

REFULING	How gracefully can teammates let go of "the way it used to be"? Can the pain of the loss be voiced and acknowledged? Can everyone see the value of the change?
REFOCUSING	How quickly do teammates embrace the new circumstances? When during the transition does the culture shift from "This hurts!" to "What's next?"

Each of these drivers of cultural wellness can be measured. Look into the future so you know which assets and liabilities each partner contributes to the merger.

CASE STUDY: GLOBAL LAW FIRM			
Challenge	Assessment	Action	Outcome
A global law firm's leadership team confronts an under-performing practice group with a faction of disengaged partners and associates.	Assessment metrics point to a breakdown of trust among teammates, resulting in an inefficient collection of individual performers who regularly bypass opportunities for collaborative business development and cross-selling.	The practice group's leader sponsors an "accountability initiative" in which behavior not aligned with organizational values is brought to the larger team for resolution. Everyone is empowered to call out day-to-day culture violations.	Within six months, natural attrition results in a new composition of talent. The team enjoys increased collaboration, cross-marketing activity and business development growth. Within two years, the team doubles in size and productivity.

THE CHALLENGE

Bad behavior gets normalized over time. When the business focus is on increasing billable hours, much gets overlooked. The unfortunate consequence of spiraling morale in this law firm was the departure of key talent. A department of 20 high-profile attorneys had shrunk to a group of 11. The remaining partners were being poached by the competition. Everyone was fielding offers.

Firm leadership had trouble explaining the trend. Team culture had grown toxic. Routine communication was tainted by unresolved resentments. Clients were beginning to take note of the turnover and lack of continuity in service. Department meetings were awkward, and little new business was coming in the door. The firm's managing partner wanted to know what was wrong.

THE ASSESSMENT

All 11 remaining attorneys participated in the team assessment survey. The results validated what everyone already knew: Toxic interchange between teammates was being tolerated and had undermined trust and collaboration. With competitive offers out there in abundance, it was easier to leave the firm than to repair and rebuild the team's culture.

Conflict scores were high. Factions had formed. Few teammates were willing to stretch themselves or take a risk on behalf of the team. Unhealthy norms had become woven into the team fabric. Incivility was sanctioned. Unless and until department leaders sponsored a full reboot of workplace mission and values, investment would remain low.

THE ACTION

The department chair called a partner meeting to share the results of the assessment and invite strategies for a solution. Those who wished to participate in the repair of the team were encouraged to suggest a vision for the group's transformation. Those who were unwilling to stand up to incivility were encouraged to seek other professional avenues.

Three partners resigned from the firm, leaving a team of eight to collaboratively redefine the department's culture. Once a new mission statement was crafted, everyone committed to adherence. Whenever a teammate regressed to an old behavior, everyone had permission to call "timeout" and confront the breach respectfully and professionally. Gradually, the workplace environment grew less tense and more supportive.

THE OUTCOME

With office politics moving in the right direction, the team was able to refocus on strategic direction. Goals related to recruitment, growth, collaboration, business development and market visibility were now possible to attain. A new crop of young associates was lured into the firm, and junior partners were empowered with new responsibility.

Executive coaching was used to support accountability for the new culture. Progress toward the new business goals was tracked and problem-solved. Within a year, the firm's reputation began to attract top talent from competitors as the department returned to its previous size and scope of services.

APPLICATION

How long does it take to transform the spirit of a workplace? Depending on the depth and duration of the struggle, employee morale can be turned around quickly. Healthy teams are always evolving their culture. Struggling teams must make a deliberate decision to change.

The tide turns long before the employee satisfaction scores rise. Mood begins to shift as soon as there is a consensus choice to challenge the norms of the organization. If most co-workers hold themselves and each other accountable to the new values, a little bit of traction is enough to instill hope for a brighter future.

Every single interaction creates an opportunity to strengthen or weaken the culture. Constructive conflict, appreciation of differences, exchanges of respect and willingness to experiment are all paths to strengthen the workplace. If teammates stay mature and professional under stress, adversity becomes a springboard for innovation and adaptability.

Each employee has a role in the process. Leaders must endorse and model actions that support wellness. Middle managers and supervisory associates are the eyes and ears of the team. Front-line staff express the success of the transformation with their engagement. Ideally, everyone acts like an owner.

Take the first step. Perform an assessment of the health and sickness of the culture. Pinpoint the most likely reasons for what ails the workplace. Perhaps the mission and vision aren't clear. Maybe trust has been broken. Some teammates may be afraid to take smart risks. Others may be depleted from the volume and pace of change in the organization.

Whatever the source of the problem, craft a plan and tackle the most impactful challenge first. Chip away at the list as positive energy returns to the workplace. Take time to acknowledge and celebrate examples of healthier culture.

The spirit of the workplace needs continuous care. It's fueled as much by words and actions as it is by silence and inaction. Steer the culture in the direction you want, with deliberate intention.

– CHAPTER 3 –

Trusting Teams

WHAT THE TRUSTING TEAM LOOKS LIKE

Trust is the secret sauce that enables teams to thrive. Once it's anchored in a relationship, growth and innovation become possible. Without it, much of the team's energy is spent managing interpersonal chaos. This is the value proposition for most teams: The less energy consumed by office politics, the more time and resources are focused on the organization's mission.

Teammates who trust each other share personal connection, respect and accountability. Teams with high trust experience closeness, acceptance, and a genuine commitment to individual and group responsibilities. Teams that lack trust tend to be closed and dismissive and lack follow-through – the symptoms of teams that are unable to use their differences, take smart risks and innovate.

As elusive as group trust may seem, there is a proven path. Psychological safety is the natural consequence when shared goals, successful conflict resolution, respect and accountability become the norms of team interaction. Each time one of these norms is tested, trust either strengthens or weakens.

Every Interaction Matters

ARE WE MOVING IN THE SAME DIRECTION?	With appreciation for the importance of team diversity, there are also certain rules of engagement that are needed to guide healthy relationships, teams and organizations. Often, these rules are expressed in the form of a mission statement where everyone agrees on values and vision. This then provides the platform for embracing the team members' differences.
DO WE UNDERSTAND EACH OTHER'S PERSPECTIVES?	Trust thrives when teammates seek to understand. Rather than struggling to get others to see your viewpoint, sponsor a culture where everyone's perception has value in the context of each person's history. Once teammates are acknowledged and validated, differences can be filtered through the agreed-upon mission according to how well they support the team's vision.
DO WE TREAT EACH OTHER WITH CIVILITY?	Very few aspects of interpersonal exchange help or hinder trust more directly than respect and disrespect. An undercurrent of disrespect forces teammates to keep their guard up and avoid smart risks. Why would anyone take the chance of expressing a novel idea when it could result in being punished, belittled, ridiculed or ostracized? Conversely, an atmosphere of kindness and unconditional positive regard promotes risk-taking and fuels innovation.
ARE WE TRUE TO OUR WORD?	Professing a belief in a mission is different than actually practicing the words and behavior that make it possible. Beyond reciting the vision statement framed on the wall in the conference room, can everyone share a story about an interaction with a colleague or client that gets to the heart of the mission? Trusting teams make integrity a high priority. Promises are kept, and deadlines are met.

Trust begins in a fragile state. Gradually, collaboration and connection strengthen the foundation of interdependence. When we rise and fall together, everyone on the team has a hand in anchoring a culture of enduring security.

KEY PAIN POINTS AND BLIND SPOTS

KEY PAIN POINT	BLIND SPOT
Undercurrent of disrespect	Dysfunctional or toxic exchange is tolerated.
Lack of accountability	Tasks have inconsistent follow-through or team norms/mission are violated.
Lack of connection	Teammates seem cautious, distant or guarded.

HOW TO OVERCOME THEM

KEY PAIN POINT: *Undercurrent of Disrespect*

Gallup's 30/50/20 metric seems to hold true in any industry. You know the breakdown. In any given workplace, about 30 percent of the employees are engaged. They would run through a wall for the organization. About 50 percent are not engaged. They're not really hurting the business intentionally. They come to work, do their jobs and collect their paychecks, but they're not the teammates you would ask to go the extra mile. And then there's the 20 percent of the team that is actively disengaged. Not all of these employees are intentionally trying to harm the workplace. Some are. But in most cases, they've simply decided to devote their energy to perpetuating toxicity.

Most business cultures try to grow the engaged group, convert the non-engaged and mitigate the actively disengaged. The engaged teammates are self-sustaining. With a small amount of investment, their energy is fueled from within.

The conversion of the middle group, a critical mass of talent, is the greatest challenge and usually tips the culture. Perhaps wrongly identified as "not engaged," these employees require a compelling vision with tangible connections. They need to have a reason for coming to work that connects with their life purpose. They must experience the place where their role makes an impact in the world. Our investment in these employees will feed succession and sustainability. These are not the obvious high-potential leaders – they are the hidden gems who, with regular mentoring and nourishment, may thrive.

The actively disengaged teammates, meanwhile, consume a considerable amount of leadership attention. Sadly, we end up devoting most of our resources to the minority of our people. Shrinking the actively disengaged group is vital.

How do you begin going about this? First, leaders are advised to allow actively disengaged workers to leave on their own rather than taking on an expensive and painstakingly slow human resources discipline policy. If an employee's psychological foundation for self-esteem requires making other people feel small, a workplace culture committed to respect and professionalism no longer feeds their fragile ego. Let your toxic employees leave and put your competitor out of business. Poisonous people seek poisonous environments.

Although the 20 percent "actively disengaged" statistic may not apply to your workplace, chances are you have dysfunctional elements lurking on your team. Most organizations do. Negative attitudes, broken personalities and poor coping skills creep from families into the job site – it's just the nature of being human. Usually, it's subtle and insidious.

In many organizations, the primary obstacle to effective, collaborative teamwork is a bullying element. Typically, a subgroup representing a small fraction of the full staff becomes entrenched in preventing change to protect their power, which they may fear is waning. Such subgroups are usually led by a few vocal, negative leaders who can get others to infect the larger organization with their message. The message takes many forms, but the theme is frequently an "us vs. them." This divisiveness makes others feel unsafe, unwelcome and unappreciated. Under these circumstances, most teammates have trouble advancing a healthier, more inclusive culture because they're made to fear the social cost they'll pay for challenging one of the bullies.

Sadly, it's easier to learn to tolerate bullying than it is to combat the poison. In simplest terms, it's theft. Time and energy that would otherwise be devoted to the mission of the organization is stolen and reallocated to keeping things broken. Managers spend countless hours putting out fires, mediating spats, soothing bruised egos and cleaning up the mess that's left behind.

So how do you combat the poison? Express unconditional positive regard for teammates. Communicate an appreciation for diversity – a diversity-friendly workplace practices respectful exchange, especially under pressure. Be willing to repair a broken connection when there has been a breach of trust. Actively communicate the values of the organization.

Negative contributors should be given a chance to get on board. Build developmental plans for those who need guidance or limits. Be detailed and clear about behavioral expectations, timelines and consequences. And don't be afraid to make a change. Elevate the engaged talent. Have the courage to move negative contributors along once they've had a chance to engage but have chosen to do otherwise. Hire slow and fire fast.

Share stories of values in action, and address violations to workplace culture promptly. Reward your engaged employees in the way they would most prefer. Coach everyone. Toxic workers are begging for limits. Under-engaged workers are asking for inspiration. Top performers crave challenges.

KEY PAIN POINT: *Lack of Accountability*

Accountability means you do what you say you're going to do. Follow through. Meet deadlines. Keep promises. Accountability also means you're true to the mission, values and vision of the organization. Ask each teammate to make an unwavering personal commitment to the rest of the group.

It's easiest for employees to practice accountability when it cascades down from the top. Integrity at the leadership level shapes the culture of the workplace, whether it's chief executives and their cabinets, superintendents and their principals, or field managers and their coaches. It's much easier to allow healthy exchange to flow down from above than it is to force a cultural transformation from the bottom up. Gravity always wins.

This doesn't mean that leadership is the sole proprietor of accountability. Everybody owns this responsibility. It's just easier for employees to hold themselves and each other accountable when it's demonstrated consistently from their leaders.

Accountability is the delicate blend of integrity and courage. Sometimes, it is as simple as following through with a commitment. Other times, it's as complex as being a consistent role model of an organization's values. Accountability isn't always measured in a performance review. Occasionally, you must ask for feedback.

Tap into the wisdom of your peers. Venture beyond the trusted insiders and pose your questions to the outsiders who have the least to lose by telling the truth. Invite your loudest partners to quiet down so your most timid collaborators can be heard. Pay closest attention to the feedback that generates the strongest emotion. Often, it's what's *not* being said that is most important.

Ask the tough questions only when you truly want the answers. Requests for feedback are often misunderstood as appeals for praise. Why ask unless you're prepared to accept the critique and make changes?

Consider intensifying the challenge. Instead of soliciting one opinion, create a feedback circle.

Feedback Circles are Useful Tools for Ensuring Accountability

Ask all teammates to prepare a strategy for continuous improvement.

Form a circle so that everyone can see each other and is a part of the same team.

The first participant shares a strategy and then listens to the feedback from each teammate, going one-by-one around the circle or interactively.

Once everyone has finished sharing their feedback, the participant summarizes what he or she heard. Then the next person in the circle presents their strategy, and the next, until everyone has had a chance to present and hear feedback from all teammates.

Empower accountability. Imagine everyone in the organization was given a referee flag so when anyone said or did something that wasn't aligned with what we all agreed to, anyone could respectfully and professionally throw the flag. Calling a penalty would be like saying, "Hey hold on a second here, I thought we agreed to these kinds of norms and this kind of collaboration. Can we get things back on track?"

KEY PAIN POINT: *Lack of Connection*

True engagement between teammates requires consistent investment. Cultures of connection are created by employees who are energized by giving rather than taking. Consider these team-building exercises as a way of strengthening connection between teammates:

- Hold an "in-common" competition. Divide teammates into small groups. Instruct the groups that they have 15 minutes to come up with as many things as possible that they share. After the time has elapsed, reassemble the full team and have a spokesperson from each group share the commonalities.
- Invite impassioned speeches. Encourage teammates to each prepare a two-minute speech on an area of personal passion. Weave these speeches into future team meeting agendas.
- Share affirmations. Have each teammate write a specific compliment about another teammate on a notecard. Teammates then share the notecards with each other via office mailbox or face-to-face.

✦   Establish a budget for team lunches or other outside-the-workplace
events. Maintain a rotating calendar of opportunities. Schedule a
team-building retreat. Escape from the trappings of the workplace
and allow team-building professionals to take care of your people.

TEAM SKILLS NEEDED FOR SUCCESS		
Listening	**Collaboration**	**Interdependence**
✓ Checking for understand-ing, clarifying discrepancies ✓ Communicat-ing uncondi-tional positive regard	✓ Joining talents ✓ Distributing workload	✓ Sharing risk/reward ✓ Entrusting individual safety to the team context

CASE STUDY: PROFESSIONAL SERVICE FIRM			
Challenge	**Assessment**	**Action**	**Outcome**
"Future Leaders" program and "Learning and Development" leaders seek to anchor the principles of effective teaming in 85 of the nation's top performing teams.	The unique demographics of each market create distinct challenges to growth and productivity for each leader. By mapping assessment metrics to business goals, there's potential to increase productivity and profit and retain more talent.	Directors and managers are trained in Team Clock® methodology and use the pre/post assessment results to craft and track actions designed to use strengths and mitigate vulnerabilities specific to each market.	A six-month team performance challenge is implemented, using weighted variables in productivity, efficiency, accountability, innovation and resilience. All 85 teams show improvement and stronger business results.

THE CHALLENGE

The conference room was packed with leaders representing financial service teams from across the nation. At first glance, all 50 teams looked alike. They were all similarly structured with operational leaders, portfolio reps and administrative support. They all shared the same business goal: to help create financial security for individuals, families and organizations. Every team aimed at the same performance targets and was provided with the same resources. Yet, the assessment of each team's performance showed significantly different results.

THE ASSESSMENT

The distinct challenges of each team ran the gamut from high turnover to employee resistance to change. Many leaders shared frustration about lack of accountability and follow-through. One courageous leader disclosed his uneasiness with the increasing diversity of his market and admitted he was struggling to adapt his business strategy. From team to team, the subjective description of "chemistry" portrayed wildly different pictures of workplace morale.

Some teams struggled to get employees engaged. Others had sacrificed the benefits of collaboration in exchange for individual performance. Many teams cited conflict resolution as their biggest challenge. Each leader shed new light on the delicate task of assembling a team and managing its growth.

THE ACTION

After each leader revealed his or her unique difficulties to the gathering of peers, the team-building workshop gradually transformed into a best-practices sharing session. Based on the customized assessment of their team's circumstances, each leader drafted an action plan aimed at addressing the specific obstacle that was impeding that team's performance. The strategies ranged from change-management training seminars to mission-anchored orientation programs for new employees.

Many leaders scheduled crucial conversations with key talent to strengthen accountability. The variability in teammate relations was wide. As such, each team wanted to improve its "chemistry." For each leader, this important driver of morale was unique to the personalities on his or her team.

Once the action plans were complete, the participants broke into feedback circles. Each leader presented his or her plan to the others in the circle and then received feedback from each colleague. Fruitful conversations unfolded.

After hearing everyone's feedback, each leader summarized key points and incorporated them into the action plan. Borrowing from the wisdom and experience of their colleagues, they were able to design strategies to improve their teams. Each plan would be implemented and evaluated by a blend of objective and subjective metrics.

THE OUTCOME

Six months later, each leader was asked to measure the impact the action plan had had on the team's performance. Objectives varied from improving the retention of job recruits to acquiring new business. The plans had included creative strategies for boosting profit, supporting growth, increasing decision speed, discovering efficiencies and reducing costs.

In each case, the leader tied his or her team-building plan to the most important business goal. All teams showed measurable improvement. And what's more: Beyond the metrics, the shift in energy and morale was palpable. A year later, a follow-up assessment showed statistical proof of sustained growth.

APPLICATION

"Team chemistry" is hard to define. Everyone knows it when they see it. Teammates appear locked in to success, whatever the endeavor might be. Colleagues anticipate each other's needs. Players play with field vision. Interdependence unfolds naturally. However, teams don't just conjure up chemistry like magic. There is a recipe.

So, what's the recipe for team chemistry? As soon as you shift from "you and I" to "we," a blend of accountability and collaboration begins to take shape. After all, what makes teams click has little to do with individual performance. It's about everyone else.

Team Chemistry Starts with a Few Basic Skills

CIVILITY NORMS	The way we treat each other matters daily and either strengthens or weakens trust.
VALUE ALIGNMENT	While we may differ on the path to the goal, we must share the same destination.
CONSTRUCTIVE CONFLICT	Disagreement, done professionally, is the lifeblood of innovation.
MEANINGFUL CONNECTION	Motivation begins with a healthy dose of caring for the well-being of others. We rise and fall together.

ACCOUNTABILITY	The most powerful drivers of interdependence are honesty, reliability, consistency and follow-through.
SACRIFICE	Distancing from the status quo and daring to take smart risks energizes a group of collaborators. The combination of fear and excitement invigorates.
LETTING GO	Growth, in any form, includes loss. Teams only evolve when they are willing to shed previously important parts in exchange for new possibilities.
EMBRACING CHANGE	As living, breathing ecosystems, healthy teams keep adapting to new circumstances. As soon as a group of people stops adjusting, that group stops growing.

As elusive as team chemistry may appear, it arises from mutual investment. Shared direction enables trust and safety. The inevitable consequence is that magical phenomenon where everyone on the team seems to be acting as one.

Once achieved, it doesn't sustain itself. Each teammate needs to morph continuously to acclimate to the new environment the team just created. Tomorrow's chemistry will not resemble the version achieved today. It's natural to get stuck while moving from stage to stage. Strong teams find a way to adapt and move forward.

CASE STUDY: ACCOUNTING FIRM			
Challenge	Assessment	Action	Outcome
Shifting from an older to a younger leadership group unveils employee factions marked by great disparity in productivity and morale, making recruitment and retention difficult.	Employees report a lack of trust in the workplace, driven by leaders' tolerance of behaviors that undermine the culture, an undercurrent of disrespect and inconsistent expectations about productivity.	Assessment results are shared in a full staff meeting, with a commitment from leadership to empower change by implementing a culture of transparency, respect and accountability.	A cultural transformation is implemented over an 18-month period, with a follow-up assessment conducted to track progress on fixing key pain points. Recruitment and retention metrics both increase.

THE CHALLENGE

Many businesses enjoy representation from many generations in the workplace. Thus, as the oldest workers plan their transitions to retirement, an eager group of future leaders waits in the wings for their chance to shape the direction of the company. After decades of people and processes operating in largely the same way at this established accounting firm, the incoming leaders (Gen-X 40-somethings) were excited to introduce some change – a different vision from that of the Baby Boomer 60-somethings. It was time to shake up the good old boys' club.

THE ASSESSMENT

To no one's surprise, the assessment metrics revealed low trust and a hesitancy to innovate. Younger workers felt disconnected from their senior partners. "Us vs. them" dynamics colored each department. Some staff reported feeling disrespected and feared negative consequences for making mistakes. Certain teammates had been "anointed" by leadership. If you weren't in the anointed group, you had to be careful. Words and behaviors that could undermine the workplace culture were often tolerated.

There were also significant differences in productivity expectations, and certain employees were not held accountable in the same way as their peers. If you were aligned with the right people, you could get away with anything.

Other than the age and experience differences between each generation of workers, there wasn't much diversity on the workforce. Not everyone felt included.

THE ACTION

The firm's partners fully understood the risks of alienating the next generation of leadership talent, but to protect the status quo, they had inadvertently damaged open communication. Before they could expect trust to improve, they would have to rebuild transparency in the culture. The first step was to call an all-staff meeting and share the assessment results.

The next step was to invite each department to revisit workplace norms. With each conversation, the inequities in expectations about performance and behavior became magnified. The new generation of leaders preferred a more consistent environment, so senior partners had an opportunity to reshape the culture. The succession plan would include more than moving people into new roles – it would also be a chance to reboot the firm's culture with greater psychological safety.

THE OUTCOME

Changes in the organizational chart were designed to provide young leaders with the power to shape the new culture. Anytime anyone said or did anything disrespectful, everyone had permission to call timeout and resolve the issue. The most senior partners in the firm agreed not to tolerate any breaches in accountability.

A handful of long-term employees decided to "retire early" as they discovered the good old boys' network no longer worked to their advantage. Even with this turnover, employee retention strengthened over the next year. The data from the follow-up assessment survey validated this transformation. In fact, a year after the original survey, scores in the areas of respect, connection and accountability had all gone up. Workplace trust had returned.

APPLICATION

Each person has different motivations for coming to work. Often, these are the things we keep to ourselves. But in an environment of respect, accountability and connection, it's safe to share these secrets. Teammates are more willing to share when trust strengthens the workplace.

Try the following **Team Accountability Exercise** if you'd like to boost transparency and accountability on your team. It's a simple, five-step exercise that unveils each teammate's contribution to the group and gives a glimpse of the motives that drive their passion for their work:

Step 1

Each teammate picks five strengths that best reflect the aspects of his or her work that drive the most energy and passion and ranks these strengths from most energizing (1) to least energizing (5). Here are some samples, though teammates don't have to stick to this list:

- Adaptability
- Analytics
- Business acumen
- Compassion
- Composure
- Competition
- Creativity
- Empathy
- Integrity and trust
- Intellectual horsepower
- Leadership
- Learning
- Priority-setting
- Problem-solving
- Strategic agility
- Teamwork

Step 2

Each teammate selects five priorities that best reflect why he or she does this work, again ranking them from strongest (1) to relative weakest (5). Ideally, our work elevates a sense of purpose and values. These five priorities should tell that story. Here are some samples:

- Compensation and benefits
- Exploration and discovery

- Growth and learning
- Helping others
- Making a difference in the world
- Prestige and recognition
- Solving complex problems
- Teaching and mentoring
- Work/life balance

Step 3

One by one, each teammate shares his or her narrative: *These are my strengths, and these are my priorities. This is what I contribute to the team, and this is why I do this work.* Put it in historical context. There's a unique story that leads to today's choices. Tell your story.

Step 4

As teammates share their stories, the other teammates offer their feedback. Does this person's narrative resonate with the words and actions you see each day? Share examples. Seize the chance to share a compliment or challenge the teammate with an opportunity for growth. Fill the exchange with respect and professionalism. Learn from others' feedback and from your own reactions stirred up by this exercise.

Step 5

Communicate a commitment to action. Notice that none of the sample strengths and priorities describe an employee who is selfish, mean, disrespectful, arrogant, unprofessional or condescending. By sharing your story, you communicate an agreement to behave in a way that reflects your best self. How will your words and actions be different after this exercise?

The exercise also gives permission for your teammates to call you out later when your words or actions are inconsistent with your professed character. Transparency and accountability are the building blocks of trust in a workplace culture, and the Team Accountability Exercise is a starting point.

CASE STUDY: CHARTER SCHOOL

Challenge	Assessment	Action	Outcome
High-performing inner-city school wishes to elevate its culture further.	Metrics from an online team effectiveness assessment reveal that accountability and collaboration are the areas where an already superior team can improve the most.	Faculty determines what the practical definitions of accountability are, and then weaves improved communication and collaboration into daily interactions.	Team effectiveness improves statistically in all Trust Stage categories.

THE CHALLENGE

Like a flower growing out of a crack in the pavement, the vibrant school building arose from an impoverished section of the inner-city, on a block that also was home to a pawn shop and a liquor store. Once inside, a visitor would no longer know the entire student population came from the local neighborhood, one of the city's lowest socio-economic areas. Paint was fresh and inspiring words adorned posters throughout the hallways. And frequently, the words on these posters were acted out in the interactions between students, teachers and administrators.

The school had already moved from good to great. There were many ways to measure its excellence. But beyond just student performance and parent satisfaction, the school's leaders, faculty and staff were interested in attracting and retaining the city's best educator talent. They wanted to move from great to greater. Continuous improvement was their mantra.

THE ASSESSMENT

The team was impressively strong in every category of measurement. Norms were clear, the mission was aligned and conflict management was effective. Interactions were respectful and teammates were connected. Diversity was embraced and the culture supported smart risks. The team was resilient in the face of change and adapted to new circumstances quickly.

The only relative weakness was accountability. Technically it didn't even measure as a weakness, scoring four out of five on the survey's five-point scale. However, with all other domains scoring between 4.2 and 4.6 on the same scale, it was the obvious area to devote attention. Still, for a team that already had consensus agreement about expectations for accountability, it would be a challenge to take accountability to a new level.

THE ACTION

The team decided to define accountability in terms of behaviors. High accountability would include proactive communication, prompt follow-through and ownership of error. Staff meeting agendas were redesigned to highlight examples of these behaviors. Specific survey questions were marked as indicators of strength in these areas. The team agreed that after a 30-day period of intentional effort to elevate these behaviors, they would reassess their trust scores.

As expected, trust scores rose in the assessment questions aimed at measuring accountability. Teammates shared anecdotes of more proactive communication, prompt follow-through and, most important, acknowledgment of the few lapses that had occurred in the chaos of running an inner-city school. They learned to thank mistakes. Whenever a teammate fell short of the culture's expectations, everyone was encouraged to express gratitude for the lessons learned.

THE OUTCOME

This school quickly became the model for partner schools in urban centers across the nation. A growing network of 183 schools now shares best practices in educating early-childhood, elementary, middle school and high school students in a nonprofit network of college-preparatory centers. Their success is rooted in an approach that emphasizes high expectations, focus on character and empowered educators.

Respect, accountability and connection become the fuel for trusting workplaces, which are able to navigate the stages of team growth with intention. They anticipate challenges and solve problems before they have a chance to take root. They understand the value of struggle and use adversity as motivation for continuous improvement.

APPLICATION

Trust supports growth. Exploration and discovery often arise from struggle. Harvard's Mind/Body Medical Institute tracks four stages of growth. These stages are aligned with the Team Clock® cycles.

Struggle (Investment Stage) – Whether teammates are frustrated, stressed or depleted, this stage is marked by not being able to solve a problem or bring relief to an unpleasant emotion. Usually, the harder we struggle, the worse the situation gets. Teams frequently struggle most in the investment phase when conflict is being negotiated.

Letting Go (Trust Stage) – Eventually, the adversity disables our ability to move forward. The impasse activates our coping skills and triggers a breakout. Teams tend to let go in the trust phase when safety permits risk.

Peak Experience (Innovation Stage) – Learning and growth unfold. New insights, increased self-awareness, creativity and rejuvenation combine to strengthen an inner platform of productivity. Teams usually enjoy such discovery in the innovation phase when they are primed to take advantage of the strength that different viewpoints empower.

New Normal (Distancing Stage) – While the stresses of the environment remain the same, we can confront them with renewed perspective and energy. Teams often recalibrate in the distancing phase after letting go of old thinking and embracing new circumstances.

Although it's uncomfortable to invite struggle into our lives, the outcome provides rich rewards. Like the moment of clarity that characterizes an epiphany, formerly insurmountable challenges become manageable. Previously laborious tasks become effortless. Allow your team to get lost. It's okay to not know the answer. You may discover a novel solution that wouldn't have been visible without the crisis.

The Trust Stage of a team capitalizes on the clarity of the Investment Stage and delivers the foundation of connection and collaboration to the Innovation Stage. Teams that create and sustain a trusting environment can endure the discomfort that accompanies growth. They can now enjoy the value of diversity and smart risk-taking that will fuel their next stage.

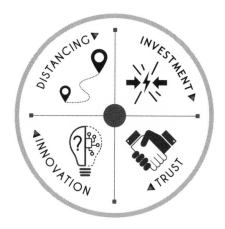

– CHAPTER 4 –

Innovating Teams

WHAT THE INNOVATING TEAM LOOKS LIKE

The comfort of the Trust Stage is sacrificed to allow risks to be taken that support innovation. Diversity norms established in the Investment Stage allow the team to take advantage of differences. Innovation activates risk-taking and allows the team to make use of its diversity. Harnessing differences stimulates dialogue, ignites collaboration and elevates the strength of each teammate.

The ability to endure the discomfort of an unknown future is critical to fostering innovative ideas. Teams that can tolerate differences and the anxiety of risk-taking are able to create, experiment, explore and invent. On the other hand, team members who don't trust each other will stick to the status quo and choose the safety of sameness over the tension of diversity.

Almost everyone performs well when there's no pressure. Many teams are at their best, however, when the pressure is high. They rise to the occasion. It doesn't matter whether it's a web designer meeting a deadline, a student taking a midterm exam or a violinist performing a recital in front of a full concert hall. Top performers become more poised when the conditions are *most* intense.

KEY PAIN POINTS AND BLIND SPOTS

KEY PAIN POINT	BLIND SPOT
Over-caution, avoiding risks	Adherence to the status quo
Lack of appreciation for different perspectives	Lack of openness to feedback

HOW TO OVERCOME THEM

KEY PAIN POINT: *Over-Caution, Avoiding Risks*

It's our natural tendency to avoid risk. When groups embark on a risk together, either the most fearless or the most fearful member of the team drives decisions. Fearless partners push their more apprehensive colleagues forward. Fearful partners pull their more confident colleagues back.

This dynamic of push and pull generates creative tension in the team that forces either growth or stagnation. Ideally, the tension supports a system of checks and balances allowing the team to move forward at just the right speed. Innovative teams recognize the benefits of the tension and harness its value.

When teams become close, the positive feelings of attachment are intoxicating. But so is the fear that overtakes optimism when something goes awry. The point is not to protect comfort. Many employees and leaders incorrectly believe successful teaming is accomplished when the employee satisfaction scores are high. On the contrary, it's not until this warm and fuzzy team is willing to sacrifice comfort that something innovative occurs.

With a foundation of connection holding the team together, courageous teammates can begin exploring growth and change. Smart risks are taken when the team decides to stretch and consider new ways of looking at old problems. Curiosity is often the fuel. Ask questions. Don't default to the safe answer. Invite all perspectives into the conversation. Innovations rarely arise from running faster or working harder. Instead, they usually result from turning things upside-down and seeing them from a different angle.

When you anchor your questions into the team's shared purpose, risks aren't likely to be harmful to the mission and vision. By considering the needs of all stakeholders, you'll take only risks that support the greater good. By challenging obsolete assumptions, you'll take the sorts of risks that stimulate new thinking.

Sample Smart Risk Exercise

Choose options from the right column (or come up with your own). Based on your choices, you can see whether you are more inclined to play it safe or stretch your growth. Rooted in your purpose, you can choose which conversations with which stakeholders should have priority.

WHAT SHARED PURPOSE ANCHORS OUR TEAM, ORGANIZATION OR COMMUNITY?	Wellness and safety Discovery and invention Wealth creation and financial stability Making a difference in the world Growth and development Fun and adventure Arts and culture Technology utility
WHO HAS INFLUENCE IN OUR INNER CIRCLE?	Teammates Shareholders Customers Employees Community stakeholders
WHAT ASSUMPTIONS SHOULD BE CHALLENGED?	Taboo topics Unspoken positions Impossible conversations Disengaged teammates
IS THERE ANYTHING WE SHOULD STOP DOING?	Obsolete tasks Bad habits Unsustainable investments Misaligned priorities Settling for "good enough" Tolerance of dysfunctional behavior

Sometimes, an "ah-ha!" moment explodes when we discover a new way to approach an old challenge. Other times, making a "stop doing" list clears space for innovation. What's on your strategic abandonment list? Two years after publishing his management book *Good to Great*, author Jim Collins shared his thoughts on strategic abandonment in a 2003 essay in *USA Today*:

"A great piece of art is composed not just of what is in the final piece, but equally what is not. It is the discipline to discard what does not fit – to cut out what might have already cost days or even years of effort – that distinguishes the truly exceptional artist and marks the ideal piece of work, be it a symphony, a novel, a painting, a company or, most important of all, a life."

KEY PAIN POINT: *Lack of Appreciation for Different Perspectives*

Innovation doesn't grow out of permission to think independently. It comes from a blending of perspectives and the chemical reactions sparked in the laboratory of a healthy culture. It comes from the delivery of your essence in every expression of your craft. It comes from the courage to be exposed. It comes from asking impossible questions about taboo topics.

In many industries, the diversity gaps widen at the leadership ranks. Gender is only one of the many forms of diversity that make an organization healthy. Strong businesses weave difference into the fabric of entry-level, middle-management and senior leadership talent tiers. Thriving teams find a way to reflect the broad demographics of their customers in the design and delivery of their products and services. The greater the leadership accountability, the more essential diversity becomes.

Diversity is the fuel for continuous improvement. Complacency is the enemy. As soon as you feel like you've created something that's never been done before, a new opportunity arises. Healthy teams don't rest on their successes. They refresh conversations with "what if" hypotheticals. They tap the diverse backgrounds and talents of their unique workforce for new ways of seeing old things.

Consider the diverse blend of talent on your team. Are the innovators appreciative of the foundation their teammates have built? Are the investors able to grant freedom to those who are energized by discovery and exploration? Can those at the bottom of the organizational chart see the vision at the top? Does everyone on the team know their role?

An easy way to spark innovation is to take "before" and "after" snapshots of the team. Ask teammates where they see themselves in relation to everyone else. Let everyone be heard.

Ask each teammate where he or she would most like to be in the future. Allow teammates to let everyone else know what they need from them in order to be successful. This is where diversity and collaboration come together.

Create your own version of the model below and spread it out in a conference room.

Invite each teammate to select a spot on the floor model that best represents their role on the team or their view of the current state of the organization. Once everyone has occupied a spot, allow the unique constellation of the team to unfold visually for everyone.

Ask each participant to answer two questions:

> *"Where are you currently on the Team Clock®?"*
> *"Why are you at this stage of the cycle?"*

Now have each participant move to the location on the model where they would most like to be. Ask each participant to answer two new questions:

"Where on the model would you most like to be in the future?"
"What would need to happen to make this possible?"

Have a debriefing with everyone who participated to acknowledge the current state of the team and determine action steps to support the team's desired future state. Track progress to ensure follow-through. Make course corrections to respond to changes.

Establish a commitment to leadership diversity in the goals and tactics of your strategic plan. Include diversity-sensitive mentoring resources in the professional development investments you make in your employees. Make sure that diversity-friendly behavior expectations are showing up across your organizational values, mission statements and performance measurements.

Innovative leaders attract open-minded talent who then collaborate in a gradual evolution of a workforce, creating new things that have value. Invention and advancement are the byproducts of a culture anchored in each stage:

Investment Stage: There's a willingness to embrace differences, encourage constructive confrontation and weave experimentation into the fabric of the team's mission and behavioral norms.

Trust Stage: Interdependence arises from accountability to the agreed-upon norms and the energizing collaboration that ensues as teammates grow closer by trading ideas, practicing respect and allowing vulnerability.

Innovation Stage: Comfort is sacrificed for excitement and fun. Teammates are willing to stretch themselves, take smart risks and even fail if it provides a lesson for future success.

Distancing Stage: Moving away from the familiar requires poise. Re-engaging in another round of creation takes resilience. Innovative teams can let go of the past and embrace an unknown future.

TEAM SKILLS NEEDED FOR SUCCESS		
Generosity	**Unselfishness**	**Compromise**
✓ Practicing open-minded kindness to others ✓ Contributing to the team without the need for recognition	✓ Practicing altruism ✓ Placing the needs of others in front of your own	✓ Appreciation of diverse perspectives ✓ Concession to support the greater good

CASE STUDY: PROFESSIONAL ASSOCIATION			
Challenge	**Assessment**	**Action**	**Outcome**
A state-based association struggles to keep pace with the growing complexity of the industry as roles and work processes transform.	Departments report having limited time and resources to support innovation despite strong desire to embrace the future with resilience.	All employees are provided with team effectiveness training and participate in a department-based assessment of strengths and vulnerabilities.	Each department implements actions to anchor trust and accountability, with the goals of creative solutions and maximized adaptation to change.

THE CHALLENGE

The needs of healthcare organizations changed dramatically over the last decade. As a primary source of education, advocacy, compliance and legal counsel to the industry, the state's professional association recognized that the traditional approach to supporting members would have to change as well. The hospital system of the future would need a far more integrated, engaged and innovative association membership.

"An Association on the Move" was launched internally as a learning and development initiative designed to rethink the traditional association model. The goal was for this association to evolve as an industry leader in supporting the members of the future in the areas of healthcare advocacy, quality, innovation and performance. To support this transformational initiative, the association committed to a 12-month assessment, training and consultation engagement. Accordingly, all employees were provided with team effectiveness training and participated in department-based assessments of team strengths and vulnerabilities.

THE ASSESSMENT

Each department participated in a pre- and post-assessment in each stage of team effectiveness. Department leaders began using coaching to improve performance. Some departments coordinated retreats to further engage their teams in the improvement process.

THE ACTION

Assessment metrics were used to create action plans to support department-specific goals. Team leaders shared evidence of collaboration where employees had demonstrated effective change management, open-mindedness, creative problem-solving and a sharp focus on the association's vision. Day-to-day interactions were characterized by higher levels of constructive conflict, appreciation for different perspectives, creative solutions to complex problems and flexibility under pressure.

Despite increasing demands on their time and resources, expected and unexpected turnover, and intense pressure to perform, association staff embraced the good-to-great culture.

THE OUTCOME

A year later, a reassessment of the team provided a pre/post comparison of progress in key areas:

Accountability to mission, vision and goals
Embracing a culture of respect and openness to diverse ideas
Celebration of creativity and innovation
Effective management of change

Overall, the association saw improvement in every department. In each area measured, the organization achieved the broad goal of anchoring a vision of accountability, diversity and innovation. This foundation would now support continuous improvement and adaptability. All departments, like the three in the example below, enjoyed positive growth in areas unique to their team dynamics.

CORPORATE FINANCE			
Investment	3.538	3.969 ↑	This team enjoys clarity about team norms, shares a common vision for the future, and is comfortable asking each other for help. Diverse perspectives remain somewhat challenging for this team.
Trust	3.521	3.943 ↑	
Innovation	3.303	3.778 ↑	
Distancing	3.432	3.859 ↑	

GOVERNMENT RELATIONS			
Investment	3.988	4.515 ↑	Diverse points of view and creativity are strongly encouraged on this team. This team challenges itself and feels empowered to achieve their goals.
Trust	4.169	4.527 ↑	
Innovation	3.952	4.444 ↑	
Distancing	4.018	4.400 ↑	

HEALTH FINANCE & REGULATION			
Investment	3.824	4.031 ↑	This team enjoys collaboration and asking each other for help. They have created a respectful culture where creativity and initiative are encouraged.
Trust	3.960	4.205 ↑	
Innovation	3.827	4.028 ↑	
Distancing	3.681	4.047 ↑	

The leadership team embraced the cyclical nature of team wellness and the key drivers of team effectiveness: mission clarity, an appreciation for difference, a commitment to respect and professionalism, accountability, openness to innovation, and the ability to discover new opportunities during change. As a result, they laid a solid foundation to support the complex and changing needs of their membership.

APPLICATION

In healthy organizations, culture change shows up in day-to-day exchanges. While the organization's vision provides a clear goal, accountability to that vision is best displayed in the daily words and actions of the individuals and teams that make up the workplace. Engaged organizations have high levels of customer satisfaction because they come up with innovative solutions to complex problems.

Action follows insight. Understanding what to do is a much different task than doing it. Unfortunately, many teams get stymied after the analysis. You can build a strategy with good intentions, but you only frustrate the team if everyone is too busy to execute. Following through with the actions arising from the assessment is the bulk of the work.

Knowing what to do is often common sense, and the analysis merely validates. It's the next steps that count. Begin with commitment. Follow with triage. Track your progress. Recognize both accomplishment and obstacles. Recalibrate to adapt to new circumstances.

- **Commitment:** We rise or fall as a team. My action or inaction directly impacts others. State your intent and guarantee achievement.
- **Triage:** The challenge is almost always greater than the resources. Break the task into a sequence of priorities. First things first, second things second. The bottom of the triage list will eventually rise to the top as new items constantly repopulate the bottom.
- **Tracking:** Milestones and timelines are only the beginning. Regular accountability meetings either acknowledge movement or ignite a problem-solving effort to address obstacles. Choose a tracking method and create transparent access for all teammates.
- **Recognition:** Taking stock in the team's accomplishments fuels the system. When the team experiences tangible movement, its motivation grows. Acknowledging barriers also is an energizer as teammates partner to solve puzzles.
- **Recalibration:** Pushing growth creates change. Strategic plans

have short shelf lives. Teams committed to continuous improvement accept the reality that they're in constant flux. Regular reassessment shifts the priorities to accommodate today's new circumstances.

The beauty of cyclical growth is the continuous chance to improve. Whether they're repairing something broken or imagining the next moonshot, teams repeat an ever-changing exercise in evolution. Those who get stuck rarely don't know what to do. They just choose not to do it.

CASE STUDY: SPORTS FRANCHISE			
Challenge	Assessment	Action	Outcome
A professional sports franchise wants to make an investment in the organizational wellness of one of its advertising sponsors.	While the routine business activity renewed each year, no actions have been taken to invest in the internal strength of partnering organizations.	The sports franchise offers to fund a team effectiveness assessment and training for this partnering sponsor as an investment in the long-term health of the relationship.	The sponsor partner accepts the gift and uses the opportunity to evaluate its readiness for innovation and growth.

THE CHALLENGE

The relationship between a professional sports franchise and its corporate partner is vital to the success of both organizations. In the traditional win-win, the franchise enjoys the benefits of the partner's capital investment, while the partner looks good in the market by way of the franchise's power. From year to year, season to season, corporate partner relationships are negotiated and renewed in the mutual interest of both parties. Retention is key.

The drivers of retention in the world of pro sports are often qualitative. Winning teams reflect brightly on the partners who purchase the rights to put their name on a jersey or a prominent location in the stadium. The reciprocal endorsement strengthens both partners and produces a return on investment, whether measured by compelling athletic performance, an excellent fan experience, tasty concessions, or state-of-the-art goods and services.

THE ASSESSMENT

The corporate partnership landscape in pro sports is intensely competitive. Most participants wage strategy in the same arena. Some sports entities, however, find innovative ways to differentiate their contribution to the relationship – not only securing an initial partnership but also greatly enhancing the prospect of retention.

At the midseason period when most franchises begin to prepare for the following season, several critical decisions are reviewed. These range from the direction of corporate strategy to the acquisition of talent to the business aspects of how to put fans in the seats who will purchase team and corporate partner products. Existing approaches are revisited, and new methods are introduced. High-performing teams empower their leaders to think outside of the box.

THE ACTION

The vice president of corporate partnerships had an innovative idea. Historically, the team had enjoyed strong retention among its corporate partners, leading to the traditional mutual benefits and return on investment. In the current challenging economic climate, however, corporate partnership renewals were not guaranteed. What was something unique that the sports franchise could do to help solidify these essential relationships?

The vice president of corporate partnerships suggested an investment in the organizational health and wellness of their corporate partners. The return on investment seemed intuitively clear: A strong and healthy organization has greater capacity to succeed in a long-term relationship than a weak and vulnerable business might. The path became clear quickly. The franchise would assemble a package of team-effectiveness services and give them to their corporate partners as an investment in their organizational wellness.

THE OUTCOME

The corporate partner's team of 25 leaders participated in the Team Clock® online assessment. The data was analyzed, revealing core strengths, vulnerabilities, and areas of consensus and disparity within the team. A week later, the leadership team participated in a training workshop where benchmarks for effective teaming were presented and the assessment metrics were debriefed. The workshop concluded with recommendations for strategic business goals based on the assessment results.

A week later, the corporate partner CEO contacted the president of the sports franchise to thank him for the investment in his organization's wellness. He described the value the exercise had created in helping his business anchor its strategic direction for the year. In the end, both organizations were comforted by the mutual commitment each business had made to the other's success.

APPLICATION

Innovation is often the solution to the struggle between capacity and complexity. The challenges that teams face get more complicated each day. The ability of the team to meet these demands is further stretched.

The gap widens as time moves forward. Depleted teammates are encouraged to work smarter, not harder. If you invest energy in designing a new way to approach a problem, you'll be rewarded by the benefits of simplicity.

The recipe seems counterintuitive: Think harder about how to get more done with fewer resources. Perhaps the innovative solution doesn't need to be manufactured. Maybe it's not a new approach.

In fact, sometimes the best path is the same strategy that solved a different problem with similar features. This is the beauty of teamwork. The wisdom usually already lives in the creative archives of a teammate's experience.

Ask these questions when facing a difficult situation:

- Has anyone ever seen something like this before?
- What approaches have succeeded and failed in the past?
- Has every teammate's voice been heard?
- Are we paying close enough attention to the outliers and contrary opinions?
- Do we have the courage to try something uncomfortable?

Take full advantage of the strength and diversity of your team. Innovation doesn't have to be a chore. Raise the voice of the quiet co-worker with the simple idea.

CASE STUDY: CONSUMER PRODUCTS COMPANY			
Challenge	Assessment	Action	Outcome
Corporate leadership of a global consumer products company must determine whether a specialty products division has what it takes to lead innovation.	Factions among teammates continue to exist after a leadership transition. Some of the more entrenched teammates still hold grudges from a merger/ acquisition 12 years earlier.	Team assessment metrics reveal the need for change management intervention so that team norms can be re-anchored to support an innovative culture. Decade-old grudges are addressed, and a foundation for collaboration is re-established.	With a foundation of mutual accountability established, team leaders model disruptive innovation by suggesting numerous product variations unparalleled in the market. Sales skyrocket and teammates begin to take greater risks.

THE CHALLENGE

Although this is a traditional company delivering expected goods to established customers, the mission of its specialty division is to innovate and attract new customer loyalty. For unexplained reasons, the team of 24 product development and marketing professionals had experienced few breakthroughs over the previous year.

Perhaps the team leader was uninspiring. Maybe the team culture lacked a foundation of trust. It was possible that the environment had somehow grown punitive for those exploring new ideas. Whatever the reason, the department needed a win, and there was little promising activity on the horizon.

THE ASSESSMENT

The team assessment survey results were concerning. For a team expected to communicate and create, there was surprisingly little collaboration. Product development, research and marketing talent had limited interaction. Those whose skills were most needed were not at the table.

Everyone had built small silos, so they could work in solitude without interference. These silos seemed counterintuitive for a team expected to explore, experiment, discover, invent and innovate. Common sense suggested everyone would want to be inside of their teammates' creative brains. Conversation was the most important tool in the toolbox and, for reasons yet to be explained, it wasn't happening.

Survey metrics revealed pockets of trust between pairs of colleagues but feelings of disrespect in group settings. The team had become risk-averse and cautious. It was clear that words and behaviors that weakened team culture were tolerated. It was normal for officemates to not greet each other, let alone pitch in on a project idea.

THE ACTION

When the assessment results were shared with the team, no one looked surprised. After all, the team had been divided since the corporate acquisition 12 years ago. An integration of cultures had never been processed. Workers had simply divided into perceived factions of "us" and "them" and focused their energies on protecting their turf. Lack of collaboration had become normal. Employees came to work, pounded out eight hours of research, design or marketing, then went home, returning the next day to the same agenda.

There was enough activity to push products forward, but nothing groundbreaking was possible under these circumstances. Too much energy was being spent on maintaining the status quo and preventing change. When the teammates realized they had a dysfunctional structure in their day-to-day existence, they vowed to fix it.

THE OUTCOME

Leaders decided to rewind the clock and go back to the team integration work that should have occurred when the acquisition was finalized a dozen years earlier. They reviewed the strengths on both sides of the merger and arrived at a consensus vision that would make best use of the diverse talent. Teammates from both sides of the "us and them" began sharing ideas and challenging each other professionally.

Everyone agreed on a fresh start as though the acquisition had just occurred. Team norms were redefined, and respectful collaboration was made a priority. Intuitive collaborations were discovered by partnering talented teammates who had previously ignored each other. Brainstorming sessions ignited organically in hallway banter, break room conversations and parking lot exchanges.

The first project produced by the "new" team was a hit. A pair of colleagues from previously different factions collaborated on the repackaging of a traditional product aimed at a younger millennial customer market. Product design specialists had fun experimenting together, and the marketing team developed a message that made a powerful splash on digital platforms. With a first win under its belt, the team had been rejuvenated.

APPLICATION

The innovations with the most impact are rarely just the good ideas arising from workplace cultures that support creativity. They are the outcomes of diversity and collaboration that begin with a problem and end with a solution that improves the world. There's a reason we unfortunately don't see more of this: As simple as the recipe might be, it's difficult to assemble a team of people who are capable of unselfish, integrative thinking.

Why, for instance, should a product designer not invite a market researcher to a business development event? Maybe the researcher can see an opportunity that lives in the designer's blind spot. Why should a bicycle manufacturer not invite a carbon fiber plant manager to a research and design meeting? Perhaps the integration of technologies might create a lighter bike frame, as well as a new customer for the carbon fiber plant. Why should a group of world-renowned physicians not invite a team of engineers and designers to a strategy session? Even though the physician has never designed a device and the engineer has never performed a surgery, the integration of their talents might create a breakthrough in disease management. Which strangers in your midst should be welcomed to your strategy session?

How Might this Apply to Your Industry?

PROBLEM IDENTIFICATION	An impasse or an obstacle creates a need for which there is not yet a clear solution.
RESEARCH	Investigation unfolds to determine current best practice or the need for a different approach.
DISCOVERY	Exploration and experimentation inevitably lead to new opportunities.

INVENTION	Fresh ideas are proposed for testing and implementation.
INNOVATION	Theory finds application, and insights become action.
IMPROVEMENT	A seemingly unsolvable problem is addressed, resulting in a better mousetrap, a cure for cancer or drastic enhancements in efficiency and productivity.

– CHAPTER 5 –

Distancing Teams

WHAT THE DISTANCING TEAM LOOKS LIKE

Distancing is a team's ability to manage change. Distancing involves either mourning or celebrating the change, accepting the change and then finding a positive way to move forward. In this stage, team members adjust to the people, process and developmental changes that have resulted from their Innovation Stage. They refocus on the new conditions that will define the direction of the next investment cycle.

Whether it's the departure of a team member, the completion of a project or a change in goals, a team needs to find a way to handle the loss so it can reposition itself and continue to be productive. Teams that distance successfully can find the time and space they need in order to adapt and replenish energy for the next phase of investment. Conversely, teams that struggle with loss and change become physically and emotionally depleted, making it difficult to reinvest in the next stage of the team's growth.

KEY PAIN POINTS AND BLIND SPOTS

KEY PAIN POINT	BLIND SPOT
Inability to transition from expressing distress to taking action	Unresolved historical personal losses are stirred up, and the reaction is larger than the current challenge warrants.
Unwillingness to embrace new circumstances and reinvest in the team	Prolonged depletion leads to burnout.

HOW TO OVERCOME THEM

KEY PAIN POINT: *Inability to Transition From Expressing Distress to Taking Action*

Every challenge has two elements – naming the source of the pain (crisis) and deciding how you're going to deal with it (opportunity). The second stage requires the first. Teams must acknowledge what hurts before they can embrace new circumstances. As quickly as you can finish trumpeting how awful a change is, commit to the task of figuring out what to do about it.

Which one of the following situations currently reflects your team? At some point, your team will face each of these challenges, as each represents a necessary stage of development in the life cycle of any group. The stuck-point comes when the discomfort of growth makes adapting difficult. The solution is to diagnose your current state, define what you want your desired state to be and keep moving.

CURRENT STATE	DESIRED STATE
Our team is new. Rules, roles and boundaries haven't yet been established.	Moving forward begins with building infrastructure. Clarify norms, expectations, mission, values and goals.
Our team is in conflict.	Set some ground rules for airing differences respectfully and professionally. Conflicting perspectives, in time, become fuel for innovation.
Our team isn't held accountable.	Both integrity and performance are dependent on teammates holding themselves and each other accountable for behavior aligned with the organization's mission, modeling its values and sharing in the achievement of its vision.

Our team is not bonded by trust.	Unless every teammate can be vulnerable, there will be a limit to the team's collective ability to take risks. A safe environment supplies the nutrients for creativity and connection.
Our team lacks the time and resources to explore and experiment.	The pinch of limits is often the spark that ignites new ideas. Rather than ramping up capacity, find a way to simplify things.
Our team has experienced significant change.	Devote time to appropriately mourn what has been lost. Look back, say goodbye and refocus on the challenges ahead. Embracing new circumstances helps to replenish energy when a team is feeling depleted.

Understanding begins with empathy. The ability to acknowledge and mourn a loss is what starts off the adaptation process. And it requires poise and clarity under pressure. Is this nature or nurture? Are leaders born with such composure, or are these learned behaviors? A little of both is the likely answer.

We acquire and develop coping skills when situations cause us to adapt. A child learning to ride a bike discovers balance just as the bike begins to tip over. If the kid's dad or mom never let go of the seat, the kid would never know to compensate to the left when the bike falls to the right. This is the beauty of struggle – it forces the need for problem-solving.

Most athletes and musicians know what it feels like to be "in the zone." Strong business leaders find the zone, too. It's that perfect blend of stress and performance that makes competency look effortless. This is a skill set that can be taught and practiced. It's basic psychophysiology. Learn the early warning signs your body communicates under stress and employ any of a variety of relaxation techniques to reboot your focus.

Managing change effectively builds resiliency. While our instincts may scream at us to avoid change at all costs, saying goodbye to the old while saying hello to the new is a reliable problem-solving method. Everything cycles if you don't waste energy staying stuck.

Here are the seven basic competencies of effective change management (adapted from *The Essentials of Managing Change and Transition*, Harvard Business School, 2005):

- **Passion:** You're excited by new possibilities.
- **Resourcefulness:** You're making the most of any situation.
- **Optimism:** You have a positive view of the future.
- **Adventurousness:** You seek to take risks and pursue the unknown.
- **Adaptability:** You have shifting expectations in the face of new realities.
- **Confidence:** You believe in your own ability to handle a difficult situation.
- **Tolerance for ambiguity:** You can live with uncertainty and surprises.

Few of us possess all of these competencies. A quick self-assessment will let you know which strengths to rely on when the going gets tough. You'll also know which weaknesses are most likely to cause you to get stuck. It's easy for teams to get stuck during periods of significant change. Energy is depleted, and emotions run high. The key is to harness the power of these normal emotions to support healthy coping and help re-energize the team.

As Seth Godin wrote in his 2012 book, *V is for Vulnerable: Life Outside the Comfort Zone*:

> *"Anxiety is experiencing failure in advance. Tell yourself enough vivid stories about the worst possible outcome of your work, and you'll soon come to believe them. Worry is not preparation, and anxiety doesn't make you better."*

KEY PAIN POINT: *Unwillingness to Embrace New Circumstances and Reinvest in the Team*

From day to day, businesses deal with changes in their industry landscape, economic conditions and personnel that require constant adaptation. Some organizations, such as school districts, pro sports teams and accounting firms, see seasonal rhythms, where business planning and talent deployment are driven by predictable changes. But other teams are more prone to unexpected changes. For example, your top salesperson accepts a job with a competitor. Or your company gets acquired, and the merger makes your job redundant. Or the economy bottoms out, and a sweeping workforce reduction is the only way for the business to survive.

The professional sports industry seems to embrace the seasonality of teams more effectively than most other business sectors. Perhaps we should take that as a lesson. In truth, most businesses, not just those in sports, enjoy seasonal cycles where predictable windows of opportunity can be used to strengthen talent and performance. The highly visible off-season changes frequently overshadow the subtle in-season adaptations that strong leaders can orchestrate. The standard business playbook may have called for the recruitment of a particular type of talent to fill some turnover gap to field the best team – but then that playbook often has to be scrapped when an unforeseen midseason disruption alters the priorities.

Unless the team's energy is spent resisting change, there are always new circumstances to address. It's one of the jobs of leaders to keep their teams moving forward. A natural friction occurs when the drain of loss meets the fuel of reinvestment. For an organization to keep up the momentum, it must respect the accomplishments of the past while inviting the possibilities of the future. The goal is to avoid getting stuck. With all due respect to history, thriving teams are the ones that move on and discover new opportunities.

The natural depletion that accompanies change is purposeful. It forces individuals and organizations to regroup. As with a night's sleep, we get a chance to recharge our batteries. What follows is a fresh look at the business landscape, a renewal of strategic direction and a re-evaluation of talent.

The most effective transitions are ones that align with a strategic plan.

Begin with a whiteboard session. Introduce a conversation about the transitions that lie ahead. Acknowledge the delicacy of the exchange, and honor it with respect for old ways, new ideas, similarities and differences.

Formalize Your Whiteboard Session with a Strategic Planning Exercise

STEP	WHAT THIS MIGHT INCLUDE
Restate the core vision of the organization.	Philosophy, mission, values, goals
Evaluate current and anticipated market conditions.	Growth opportunities, specialization/branding, local/national/global market changes, talent/succession, revenue/funding, space/resources
Identify key areas of strategic focus.	Strategy-aligned recruitment, employee development, research/innovation, business growth/marketing
Develop a strategic framework to support the organization's vision.	Mission/culture, business/revenue needs, innovation opportunities, succession and recruitment needs, organizational excellence
Assign tasks and timelines to ensure accountability.	Gantt chart or similar tracking method and follow-up procedure to ensure accountability

Commit to continuous evaluation of your team's circumstances.	✓ Are the goals still appropriate? ✓ Has any technology affecting operations changed? ✓ Are there any other key areas that now need to be added to our strategic direction? ✓ What is working well? What is not working well? ✓ Are there any new industry, marketplace, compliance or regulatory issues that will affect the way we do business? ✓ Are the ongoing evaluations providing the information needed? Is this information being used to improve the processes?

Healthy teams have a thread running from vision to execution. Goals need strategy. Strategy requires tactics. Tactics dictate action. Action demands accountability. Accountability forces timelines. Timelines help to define measurement. Each teammate needs to know where he or she fits in the following series of challenges:

Where are we going (vision)?	While all voices may not be equal, every teammate has a voice in the direction of the team.
How should we get there (strategy)?	There are many paths to the same destination. Plan from many viewpoints.
What is the best route (tactics)?	First things first. Use a triage method to choose the course with the greatest urgency, then chip away at the lower priorities.

What steps are required (action)?	Each tactic has multiple stages. Break the action down into bite-sized sections. Sometimes, momentum is easier with breaks between spurts of activity.
Who will take ownership of each step (accountability)?	The roles of each teammate are linked. Transparency and communication provide a connection between the smallest action and its contribution to the vision.
When should each phase be completed (timelines)?	Deadlines influence pace. Whether teammates prefer to be proactive, steady or last-minute, adhering to a timetable is a form of respect between teammates.
How will we know we've accomplished the goal (measurement)?	The movement from current state to desired state should be quantified. Subjective goals with squishy milestones are rarely motivating. Keep a scorecard.

Because of the continuous nature of change, you'll need to pay constant attention to the shifting circumstances of your team. Anticipating these changes means you can craft a proactive response rather than having to scramble when it's nearly too late. Seize the opportunity to rethink team norms and recommit to the team's mission.

Trust and collaboration are strengthened by this process. If the Distancing Stage is managed well, the team enjoys another cycle of discovery and innovation. The lessons learned from the last period of change are applied to the management of the next phase. Once again, the team is revitalized.

TEAM SKILLS NEEDED FOR SUCCESS		
Sacrifice	**Delay of Gratification**	**Coordination**
✓ Surrendering individual needs to move the group forward ✓ Acknowledging and accepting loss/failure as a team	✓ Forgoing immediate satisfaction for long-term gain ✓ Patience with the differing paces of teammates	✓ Orchestration of diverse players and variables ✓ Harmonizing disparate voices

CASE STUDY: ACADEMIC MEDICAL FACULTY			
Challenge	**Assessment**	**Action**	**Outcome**
A change in faculty leadership results in old guard vs. new guard factions.	A faculty mutiny is fueled by protesting physicians who are demanding that the new leader be replaced.	A majority of teammates respond to the gauntlet by collaborating on a refreshed vision that reflects the new leadership direction.	Within six months of the assessment, 10 percent of the faculty leave the department for other opportunities. The recruitment efforts that follow spark international competition to be part of the team.

THE CHALLENGE

University-based medical teams are typically stocked with esteemed faculty who have recently discovered a breakthrough technique or published a best practice. Often, brilliance and competitiveness have paved the way for their success. These team members earned the highest MCAT scores, got into the best medical schools and secured the most prestigious residencies and fellowships. Academic hospitals and medical colleges work hard to attract and retain these special talents.

However, there's a common drawback: Despite their rare skill sets, these physicians don't always play nice in the sandbox. They can be selfish and sometimes arrogant. Once they're a part of a medical facility delivering care, they're expected to be cooperative and collaborative with the other specialists who make up the multidisciplinary team. When they don't get along with their peers, it becomes difficult for the team to deliver care, advance research, recruit world-class talent and educate the next generation of physicians.

THE ASSESSMENT

This medical faculty team struggled to move the department forward with clinical excellence, recruitment, research and business development strategies. Assessment data revealed stymied efforts at change management, a lack of alignment on the direction of the department, broken trust and an undercurrent of disrespect in teammates' day-to-day professional exchanges. Much of the team's energy was being spent on infighting as they protested the university's expectations and the department chair's vision.

Faculty meetings were free-for-alls. A small faction – about 20 percent of the department – had redirected their energies to getting rid of the department chair. Time that should have been dedicated to advancing the department was instead spent huddling in the ringleader's office plotting strategy to disrupt. These team members had the ear of the dean of the medical college, so they felt empowered.

THE ACTION

With considerable difficulty, the remaining 80 percent of the department attempted to build a team culture that would support their efforts to achieve the university's expectations for growth and clinical excellence. Younger faculty grew tired of the mutiny. In a courageous action, a few strong future leaders stood up to the vocal minority, challenging the motives of the naysayers. They expressed their desire to move forward rather than staying stuck and rehashing the same complaints over and over.

The protesting faction was invited to either participate in the group's new direction or step out of the way of progress if they preferred to resist. In a key moment at a pivotal faculty meeting, the department chair asked the resisters to either join the rest of the team in embracing the plan for growth or excuse themselves from the room. This was the second meeting of this type and, like the first time, the chair had reserved a separate meeting room to which the resisters could excuse themselves immediately, if that was their choice. This time, all but one stayed.

Although the ringleader had chosen to silently stay in the first meeting, this time she expected her followers to join her as she walked out. But no one did. The room was awkwardly quiet for about a minute, and then the meeting got underway. Each agenda item – clinical excellence, recruitment and retention, education and training, marketing visibility, business growth – was discussed without hostile interruption, and with participation from the entire room.

THE OUTCOME

The renewed team agreed to begin chipping away at each strategic priority. As expected, productivity and clinical outcome metrics improved. The ringleader of the resistance decided not to stay with the university. Additionally, one of her followers left to join her in her new opportunity. Everyone else got on board as new medical processes and efficiencies were discovered and new talent from competing medical groups interviewed for a chance to join this freshly enthusiastic team.

A year later, the courageous young faculty members who had challenged the naysayers were promoted to department leadership roles based on their contributions to the team's positive growth. The department chair's authority was fully embraced by the dean of the college of medicine. As the chair reflected on the change in her team's effectiveness, she described the department as "humming" and "raising the bar of professionalism."

APPLICATION

Not all teams experience the pleasure of moving from good to great and becoming a magnet for the world's best talent. The lucky few organizations spend countless hours chipping away at the elements that threaten to erode employee morale and client satisfaction. They know the job is never complete, and they operate in a continuous improvement mode. But most teams go through more onerous cycles of loss and change. Workplace energy is depleted. Factions develop. There's disagreement about vision and goals. An undercurrent of disrespect undermines trust. Accountability slips. Teammates are afraid to serve up innovative ideas.

Eventually, the landslide begins. Someone finally has enough and abruptly departs. The bold move is contagious, and suddenly everyone is thinking about other career options.

Here lies the threshold of opportunity. While inertia and momentum virtually guarantee the team will enter a new cycle just like the old one, courageous leaders call timeout and rethink direction. The path is arduous, but the steps are clear:

1. Name the pain. Diagnose the symptoms and acknowledge the team's sickness.
2. Decide whether to stay stuck or move forward. Those who prefer to stay stuck should respectfully excuse themselves from the team.
3. Get the remaining team in agreement on a refreshed statement of mission, values and vision.
4. Make an accountability pact in which everyone agrees to assist each other in staying true to the desired workplace norms.
5. Use every interaction as an opportunity to strengthen the culture moving forward. Missed opportunities, by default, weaken the team.

As with most change, the situation needs to become intolerably painful before it sparks transformation. Until that moment, it's easier for teammates to normalize the discomfort and find a sympathetic ear for their complaints. Commiserating generates energy, albeit negative energy. Once the team is finished railing at the sky about how awful the situation is, healthy actions can begin.

CASE STUDY: SCHOOL DISTRICT			
Challenge	Assessment	Action	Outcome
Faculty surveys reflect harmful factions in the school culture, highlighting concerns about teacher-teacher and teacher-principal relations. A change-resistant vocal minority is making it difficult for the faculty to move forward as a unified team.	100 percent participation in the Team Clock® online assessment reveals both assets and liabilities.	Based on the foundation of a common vision, staff and leadership are challenged to practice accountability in their words and behaviors.	A "peer culture advisory panel" is assembled to represent full staff concerns. Gradually, teammates' interactions increasingly reflect the organization's ideal culture goals.

THE CHALLENGE

A small faction of workplace bullies had assumed power in the wake of a leadership change. At the outset, the behaviors dividing the team were subtle. But over time, the culture took on the spirit of a high school cafeteria, with cliques determining whether you were in or out of the club. Trust was an issue, and staff reported being unable to speak freely among their peers without risking retribution.

The signs and symptoms were everywhere. A young employee would serve up a fresh idea in a staff meeting, only to be dismissed with an eye-roll and a scoff by one of the bullies. Project opportunities were doled out according to political position rather than merit. Gossip replaced direct conversation as teammates grew less likely to take risks with sensitive matters. Those brave enough to embrace the direction of the new leader were ostracized as disloyal to the outgoing boss. The status quo needed to be protected. Change was the enemy.

THE ASSESSMENT

Workplace culture surveys revealed the obvious: Disrespect was tolerated. Trust was low. Mistakes were met with punitive consequences, resulting in an unwillingness to innovate. Staff turnover was at an all-time high, leaving the human resources recruiter constantly searching for replacement talent, with little likelihood of retaining the best and brightest.

There were some positives. Specifically, these strengths were noted:

✓ Leaders receptive to candid feedback
✓ Encouragement of initiative and creativity

Meanwhile, the vulnerability themes creating opportunity for the team included:

✓ An insufficient foundation of healthy norms
✓ An undercurrent of disrespect
✓ Hesitance to confront inappropriate behavior
✓ Intolerance of differences in perspective
✓ Discomfort asking each other for help

THE ACTION

The new leader was forced to make rudimentary changes in personnel and culture. The bullies would need to be confronted head-on. Their future roles would be tied to their ability to manage day-to-day interactions with colleagues in a professional manner.

She would begin with basic training around conflict-resolution skills. She would take a more active role in holding teammates accountable for interactions that embraced diversity as a strength. And she would establish and train a peer culture advisory panel that would be charged with the following:

✓ Receiving input from the staff about relevant, fixable issues
✓ Recommending actions to address any obstacles to living the vision consistently
✓ Serving as a mediation panel for conflicts unable to be resolved through direct conversation and traditional support

Whenever interactions hinted of disrespect, teammates were empowered to invoke the professional standards of the mission, values and vision statement they had unanimously adopted. Gradually, the teammates whose behavior most matched up with the vision assumed leadership roles. Those who were more resistant to change were slowly neutralized by a strengthening workplace that was less tolerant of words and actions that didn't resonate with the new culture.

THE OUTCOME

It took about six months for employees to begin noticing the culture shift. Only one of the bullies chose to leave as his peers became decreasingly tolerant of his adolescent methods. Meanwhile, this bully's formerly most loyal henchman seized the chance to become a leader by embracing the new culture and doing his best to influence others to do the same.

Gradually, the staff chipped away at an ever-shrinking list of unresolved issues, either through private conversation, advocacy from leaders or mediation from the peer culture advisory panel. The school year ended with an optimistic outlook for the start of the next one. A mechanism is now in place for managing future challenges with professionalism, fairness and respect.

APPLICATION

Even a handful of unhappy teammates will suck energy from the workplace. This is contagious and pervasive. For any healthy team, the less time and effort spent on workplace politics, the greater the focus on the mission of the organization. What you tolerate, you sanction. Every workplace has a few disengaged employees; don't give them permission to define the culture with unhealthy words and actions.

Changing the culture of a workplace can take a long time. Basic science tells us that living things seek sameness. Even a loosened violin string will tighten itself back up. The longer the history of broken morale, the harder it is to set a new mood. Unless the desired future is enforced consistently, old ways slip back into place. The Distancing Stage is the team's opportunity to regroup, recharge and refocus.

– CHAPTER 6 –

Next Steps for Achieving Breakthrough Teams

The cycles of teams have distinct stages. We *invest, trust, innovate* then *distance* to regroup and repeat the cycle. New opportunities unfold at each of the four stages. The following questions will help ensure your team makes the most of each chance:

Investment Stage

+ Are we aligned in a common vision?
+ Have we been true to the mission and purpose of our work?
+ Do we embrace conflict and differences in perspective in a professional way?

Trust Stage

+ Have we fed and nourished our partners?
+ Do we hold ourselves and each other accountable?
+ Can we collaborate in ways that increase productivity and make us more efficient?

Innovation Stage

+ Have we reserved time for creativity in our daily routines?
+ Are we courageous enough to challenge the status quo?
+ Are exploration and discovery supported by our leadership?

Distancing Stage

+ Have we found lessons in our mistakes and let go of past regrets?
+ Can we adapt effectively after disappointment?
+ Are we able to remain poised, nimble and focused during change?

In today's business climate, only the most engaged, committed, innovative and adaptable teams survive and thrive. When you make your teams more effective, you improve the wellness of your partnerships. The results appear in both your personal and professional circles.

Make the investment. Diagnose the challenge. Understand the value of struggle. Find the courage to overcome the obstacles.

Team Clock® is dedicated to elevating teams through proven clinical methodologies, providing a simple path to healthy, thriving teams and organizations. Teams can become dysfunctional, creating chasms that negatively affect morale, talent retention and the success of the business. Often, business or human resources leaders recognize the problem but can't fix it, either because they don't know how or because they haven't been empowered within their organizations. The goal is to keep moving forward. Advance to the next cycle by applying these simple steps:

STEP 1: *Commit to a Healthy Workplace Culture.*

Clarify mission, values and vision.	When everyone agrees on the "what," the "how" and the "where," you then have a checklist with which you can filter all future words and actions. Without this consensus, anything goes. Get clear about norms, roles, rules and boundaries.
Endorse respectful difference of opinion.	The richness of difference should be built into the norms. If everyone agrees to act like mature and responsible adults, constructive conflict has the potential to fuel exciting growth.
Embrace shared accountability.	Even if some members of the team can self-police their words and actions, a referee is often needed to remind those who slip that we all agreed to a respectful set of norms. Call yourself out when you say or do something that hurts the culture. Call your teammates out when you see it in others. Ignoring regression – either accidentally or intentionally – sanctions the return to previous broken ways.

Practice new behaviors collaboratively.	Every time a collaboration that models agreed-upon values takes place, a new root is sent down to help anchor the organization. While initial efforts might begin awkwardly, repetition eventually makes respectful interchange a normal part of working.
Celebrate evidence of change.	Tell stories of success. Begin each staff meeting with a moment about the mission. Describe an exchange with a co-worker or client that illuminates the organization's mission, values and vision. Make it real by recognizing what has changed and rewarding courageous behavior.
Adapt for continuous improvement.	Avoid complacency. Improvement alone does not mean a job is complete. All relationships, teams and organizations cycle through phases of growth. The successful elevation of a workplace culture creates a platform for the next level. Go from good to great. Move from great to greater. The cycle only ends when the team chooses to stop adapting.

STEP 2: *Identify What Stage You're In.*

Go beyond the book and take the Team Clock® online assessment at *www. centerforteamexcellence.com.* The survey includes 40 questions and takes about 15 minutes to complete. You'll receive a baseline of data about how your team communicates, manages conflict, honors accountability, collaborates, uses its differences, takes risks, deals with adversity and handles change. All individual responses are confidential and managed by the Center for Team Excellence. Data is summarized in aggregate and shared with leaders (individual responses are not shared). These metrics provide the foundation for goal-specific actions, training and coaching.

The Team Clock® solution is a powerful framework that transforms teams. It starts with an assessment to diagnose strengths, weaknesses and vulnerabilities. Using the data, the Center for Team Excellence provides training on effective team functioning, as well as individual and group coaching. If you don't have the right human resources talent in your organization, Center for Team Excellence consultants offer specialization in interpreting data, training in team effectiveness and coaching leaders across a spectrum of industries.

STEP 3: *Use the Other Resources at the Center for Team Excellence Website.*

The site is stocked with tools and resources to assist organizations seeking to repair or enhance workplace culture. Begin by meeting our team of founders, certified consultants and advisory board professionals. Take some time to look over our methodology section, where you'll find an hour-by-hour explanation of the Team Clock® model. The clients and testimonials section will highlight case studies across many industries, including business, education, financial services, healthcare, not-for-profit, performing arts, professional services, real estate, retail and sports. The media section contains numerous audio and video clips from recent training sessions, as well as downloads and award recognitions. And the solutions section connects you to team wellness packages, books, trainings and coaching resources.

In addition, the Center for Team Excellence blog is an easy-access clearinghouse of team wisdom where you'll find archived insights and recommendations on the following topics:

- ✓ Best practices in team effectiveness
- ✓ Change, growth and succession
- ✓ Collaboration and communication
- ✓ Continuous improvement
- ✓ Diagnosis and assessment
- ✓ Engagement and trust
- ✓ Innovation
- ✓ Interpersonal relationships
- ✓ Leadership

- ✓ Networking
- ✓ Organizational excellence
- ✓ Team cycles
- ✓ Team wellness
- ✓ Workplace culture

Finally, you can connect with certified Team Clock® consultants, who have workplace culture assessment tools to help you anchor mission/values/vision, sustain team trust, spark business growth and innovation, and help your organization to be resilient through change. These consultants bring solutions to life through a combination of assessments, on-site trainings, coaching and action-planning, drawing on their industry specialization in higher education, human resources, marketing, operations, healthcare, human services, legal services, professional athletics and financial services.

STEP 4: *Share What You've Learned. Get Your Team to Speak the Same Language.*

Share this book – this simple model provides a common language for all teams that you can spread throughout your organization. Encourage regular assessment. Involve teammates in strategic action-planning (*view table on next page*).

Everyone in your organization should be able to answer these questions.

Where are we on the Team Clock®?	What stage are we in right now? Investment? Trust? Innovation? Distancing? What are our pain points? Some examples: ✓ Healthy team norms ✓ Mission alignment ✓ Constructive conflict ✓ Mutual respect ✓ Shared accountability ✓ Connection and cohesion ✓ Using differences as strengths ✓ Risk-taking ✓ Appropriate mourning of loss, failure or disappointment ✓ Refocusing on new circumstances
Why are we in this stage of our team's growth?	Are we going through a change now? Have we just come out of a change? Do we need to re-anchor our vision? Do we need to hold each other and ourselves more accountable to the goals and values we all agreed to? Do we need to get out of our comfort zone in order to be more innovative? Do we need to take stewardship of a transition and make sure it's healthy?
What actions should we be taking to move the team forward?	What do we need to work on first? Is it conflict? Do we need to be better at change management? Do we need to build more trust? Do we need to be more accountable? Are we aligned with our mission?

STEP 5: *Apply the Model to Personal, Family, Social and Community Settings, Where Teams Also Thrive.*

Although many of us spend most of our waking hours at work, the workplace is not the only place where we face team challenges. The same principles that make work teams successful apply to any relationship. Marriages, friendships and other interpersonal relationships navigate the same four stages. Let's revisit the marriage example. In the Investment Stage, couples are discovering each other. In the Trust Stage, they're becoming more intimate. In the Innovation Stage, they're testing out new adventures. In the Distancing Stage, the relationship requires some space to adjust to changes. At each stage, the investments, connections, risks and losses are different as the relationship grows.

Many people also participate in clubs, recreational sport teams, community organizations and faith congregations. The wellness and success of these experiences evolves as teammates negotiate norms, set goals, manage conflict, build trust, create change and adapt to shifting membership. No matter the form a team takes, it's always good to ask where we are, why we're there and where to go next. Team Clock® provides the framework to do just that.

FINAL THOUGHTS

The ability to collaborate effectively within teams is one of the greatest tests of communication. Growing up, most of our education is skewed toward individual success. We learn to set goals, take initiative and budget our time based on our own pace and work ethic. We assume that applying the same rubric will lead to success in team settings – that strong individual performance, along with respect for others, constitutes teamwork. Not always. In fact, it might even be a detriment.

Exceptional individual performers frequently struggle in teams. Even seasoned leaders often cite the management of teams as the most challenging part of their job. For many, climbing over the back of your colleague is the most direct path to success. Utilitarian goals (i.e., the greatest good for the greatest number of people) run contrary to the standard recipe for individual gain. To have both effective cooperation and productive conflict requires an unusual blend of sacrifice.

Communication in teams begins with a different rulebook. It starts with the understanding that teams are messy. Conflict is unavoidable. Dynamics depend on the unique circumstances, mindsets and emotions of the team members involved. Graduate programs routinely teach the 1965 Tuckman Forming-Storming-Norming-Performing model, yet teams often skip key stages and regress under pressure.

The human element drives the culture of the team more powerfully than theory does. It only takes a couple of actively disengaged teammates to start a mutiny. One distracted collaborator can hijack the agenda of a meeting. Selfishness disguised as altruism can undermine a mission.

Collaboration in team settings is cyclical. As the team evolves from stage to stage, communication and behavior shifts to accommodate ever-changing circumstances.

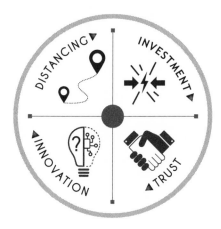

Investment Stage

- *Take stewardship of team norms by owning the way teammates are treated.*
- *Align everyone to the team's mission, vision, values and goals.*
- *Sponsor mature, constructive conflict to maximize the strength of diversity.*

Trust Stage

- *Demand respect in all interactions, especially during stressful times.*
- *Own accountability to agreed-upon norms, mission and goals.*
- *Nurture connections between teammate; collaboration fuels a greater good.*

Innovation Stage

+ *Use the fuel of differences to spark creativity.*
+ *Take the smart risks that support change and growth.*

Distancing Stage

+ *Let go of the urge to keep things the same for comfort's sake.*
+ *Embrace the re-energizing nature of new challenges.*

Rules change when we move from a "me" to a "we." Goals are co-owned. Trust is a fragile yet non-negotiable requirement. The stakes are raised because of the precious cargo on board in the form of teammates. Change impacts the whole team. As with a family, all transactions happen with a clear understanding of the effect on each member. Only together do we move forward.

– AFTERWORD –

As the founder of the Center for Team Excellence, I have reached my 64th birthday, partnered in a 41-year marriage, helped to raise three children toward a successful transition to adulthood, welcomed grandchildren into the family team, worked for four thriving organizations and launched two businesses. Each of the elements of my life has spiraled through dramatic cycles of growth and transformation. The level of investment deepens with each cycle. Conflicts require increasingly complex resolutions. The depth of trust intensifies. Connections strengthen. Discoveries bring added excitement. Losses and disappointments hurt more profoundly. New opportunities produce unmatched joy.

Whatever group of partners defines your team, each day is a chance to evolve. Continuous improvement requires constant reassessment. How are we doing? Are we together in this goal? Do we need a course correction? Is anything broken that needs fixing? Is this our best? What might happen if we pushed the limits? Have we had a chance to recover from the recent changes? What lies ahead?

This is the beauty of teams. They are complex and simple at the same time. Human interaction is unpredictable, yet the stages of development are predictable. The richness of relationships lives in every connection. Whether it's a trusted mentor or a stranger who has crossed your path, the exchange is shaped by your ability to invest, your capacity for trust, your appetite for innovation and your need for distancing. Visible or not, these variables are always at play.

Consider *The 4 Stages of a Team* a call to action. Look at every relationship and team that matters in your life. Assess the strengths and opportunities of each connection. Decide what aspect of each team needs the most attention. Design an action plan to address the highest priorities. Follow through with your commitment to improve the team.

In its purest form, teamwork is a commitment to use your power to elevate someone else. At its best, the commitment is mutual, and it deepens over time. When we thrive, we have companions with whom to celebrate. When we falter, there's always another chance to make things right. Cycle after cycle, stage after stage, the choice to reinvest keeps partnerships growing toward the comfort of the familiar and the excitement of the unknown.

– ACKNOWLEDGEMENTS –

When you interact with people closely, a piece of them gets inside of you and gets carried forward into everything you do. It's a version of eternity. The ripple effect of the chemistry you have with others changes your DNA and that of everyone who connects subsequently. The following friends and colleagues are now a part of my makeup, and I'm excited to deliver their influence to the future. Pieces of them are woven into this book, which would not have been possible without their direct and indirect contributions.

When you read this book, you will have the pleasure of getting to know Maryanne Adams, Nancy Alonso, Mawi Asgedom, Harold Baines, Jessica Barnes, Clay Baznik, Wes Becton, Fred Behm, Brian Blaha, Rose Burpo, Jan Clavey, Andy Corbus, Rich Dayment, Aline Defiglia, Flint Dille, Tessa Flaherty, Michelle Flowers, Josh Gaby, Kerry Galarza, Megan Guenther, Ozzie Guillen, Susan Heitsch, Roland Hemond, Anthony Holmes, Mark Kelly, Monica Kerber, Weykyoi Victor Kore, Scott Malaga, Abby Marshall, Lauren McGuire, Corey McQuade, Michael Melbinger, Cara Milianti, Kim Morris-Lee, Craig Niederberger, Bryan O'Donnell, Beth Plachetka, Steve Reff, Tim Ressmeyer, Lisa Rexroad, Dave Schmidt, Ann Schreiner, Amy Schryver, Lisa Schvach, Valerie Scislowicz, Emily Shelton, Michelle Sherbun, Rachel Shuty, Mary Stephenson, Michael Tahlier, Lori Tompos, Katie Twohy, Ron Watkins and Barry Wenig.

To all of you, thank you for your influence, mentorship, support, patience, wisdom, courage and insight.

- RESOURCES -

What Google Learned from Its Quest to Build the Perfect Team
https://www.nytimes.com/2016/02/28/magazine/what-google-learned-from-its-quest-to-build-the-perfect-team.html

The New Science of Building Great Teams
https://hbr.org/2012/04/the-new-science-of-building-great-teams

Yale Center for Emotional Intelligence
http://ei.yale.edu/

Harvard Business Review: Measuring the Return on Character
https://hbr.org/2015/04/measuring-the-return-on-character

Harvard Business Review: Building the Emotional Intelligence of Groups
https://hbr.org/2001/03/building-the-emotional-intelligence-of-groups

Human Capital Institute study: The Three I's in Effective Teams: Intention, Interaction and Influence
http://www.hci.org/hr-research/three-effective-teams-intention-interaction-and-influence

Gallup State of the American Workplace
https://www.gallup.com/workplace/238085/state-american-workplace-report-2017.aspx

– ABOUT THE AUTHOR –

Steve Ritter is an internationally recognized expert on team dynamics whose clients include Fortune 500 companies, professional sports teams, and leading education, healthcare and professional service organizations. He is on the faculty of the Center for Professional Excellence at Elmhurst College where he earned the President's Award for Excellence in Teaching. Steve's unique blend of training in the worlds of human resources, organizational development and psychology inspired the creation of the Team Clock® methodology, an approach that merges the business and clinical fields to empower growth of teams. He is the acclaimed author of the 2009 Amazon Top 50 Business Book: *Team Clock: A Guide to Breakthrough Teams* and the 2014 release: *Useful Pain: Why Your Relationships Need Struggle.*

Made in the USA
Columbia, SC
26 June 2019